Smoky SPANISH-STYLE Grains & Rice

Spicy MEXICAN-STYLE Grains & Pulses

100% QUINOA Red & White Simply Cooked

Zingy KOREAN-STYLE Grains

PUY

100% QUINOA Red & White Simply Cooked

Pesto-ey ITALIAN-INFUSED Grains

Aromatic PERSIAN-STYLE Quinoa & Lentils

Spicy CAJUN-STYLE Lentils & Red Kidney Beans

PUY LENTILS Simply Cooked

Smoky SPANISH-STYLE Grains & Rice

GLORIOUS GRAINS with Red Rice & Quinoa Simply Cooked

BELUGA LENTILS Simply Cooked

KOREA

Zingy KOREAN-STYLE Grains

100% QUINOA Red & White

Pesto-ey ITALIAN-INFUSED Grains

PUY LENTILS Simply Cooked

MERCHANT
GOURMET

THE SIMPLE
PLANT-BASED
COOKBOOK

AN APPETITE FOR CHANGE WITH
LENTILS, GRAINS AND CHESTNUTS

Recipes by Kitty Coles
Photography by Kim Lightbody

Hardie Grant
QUADRILLE

CONTENTS

AN APPETITE FOR CHANGE

Merchant Gourmet are on a mission to help as many people as possible discover the true pleasure of plant-based food and to eat less meat.

We know that the concept of saving the environment can feel overwhelming, so we have created this cookbook to show you that there is an easy and delicious way!

Now you can stand up for the environment by sitting down to a delicious and easy-to-prepare plant-based meal.

PLANT-BASED SIMPLICITY

We believe that eating food that is better for your health and better for the planet should never be at the cost of time or taste. So we want to keep things as simple as possible. Simple products and ingredients that come straight from Mother Nature. Simple recipes that break down plant-based cooking to make it easy to achieve, every day, using lentils, grains and chestnuts. Most importantly, a simple way to help save the planet, one great meal at a time!

We hope you have as much fun with this book as we had making it, and that it inspires your appetite for change. If it does, we invite you to join us and help lead the change you want to see.

Find out more at **www.merchant-gourmet.com**

WHY PLANT-BASED?

"There is no doubt we will not tackle the climate crisis until global meat consumption is reduced and we know that it can seem intimidating to those trying to eat plant-based for the first time. As a long-term supporter of Veganuary, Merchant Gourmet has been the catalyst for many people starting their plant-based journey, by providing a quick and easy way to make delicious plant-based meals with natural ingredients that are both good for us and good for the planet."

Ria Rehberg, CEO of Veganuary

VEGANUARY

16 MILLION CARS

If everyone in the UK replaced one
more red-meat meal per week with a
plant-based dish, it would reduce the
UK's greenhouse gas emissions by
50M tonnes, the same as taking
16 million cars off the road.

THE FUTURE OF FOOD IS THOUSANDS OF YEARS OLD

LENTILS

Lentils are a real gift from Mother Nature in plant-based recipes! High in protein and fibre and counting as one of your '5 a day', lentils can be easily swapped for mince and other meat in many of our favourite recipes.

Clockwise from top right: A Twist on Moussaka (page 71); Falafels with Hummus & Flatbreads (page 112); Tomatoey Lentils & Beans on Toast (page 47).

CHESTNUTS

Chestnuts and chestnut purée make the perfect dairy replacement in so many plant-based desserts and savoury dishes, as well as adding an extra depth of chestnutty flavour! They're also a great source of fibre and add a rich texture to the dishes they're used in.

Clockwise from top right: Chocolate & Chestnut Torte (page 143); Tomato & Caper Tart with Chestnut Tapenade (page 108); Chestnut & Banana 'Ice Cream' (page 145).

QUINOA

Technically a seed, quinoa is not only an excellent source of protein and fibre, its light, fluffy, pliable texture means it can be used in so many plant-based recipes in so many different forms. It also carries flavour brilliantly.

Clockwise from top right: Quinoa Veggie Balls (page 58); Quinoa Apple Pie (page 149); Quinoa, Apple & Herb Salad (page 25).

WHOLEGRAINS

We have a variety of wholegrains within the Merchant Gourmet range, from red rice to wheatberries and black barley to freekeh. We hate seeing grains relegated to the side of your plate as a bulking ingredient! After all, they're a great source of fibre, which we're often lacking in our diet.

Clockwise from top right: Italian Grain Arancini Balls (page 115); Smoky Spanish Wholegrain Paella (page 84); Fennel, Pea & Courgette Soup (page 33).

Light Meals
& Quick
Lunches

ORANGE, ROCKET & FENNEL SALAD
WITH SPANISH-STYLE GRAINS

In summer, this is the perfect quick lunch. Segmenting
the orange is so worth it for the pockets of sweet citrus.

 SERVES 2   10 MINS

INGREDIENTS

- 1 medium orange
- Small handful of almonds
- 1 x 250g pouch of ready
  cooked Smoky Spanish-Style
  Grains & Rice
- 50g rocket
- 1 small fennel bulb, halved
  and very thinly sliced
- Handful of parsley leaves

For the dressing
- 1 tbsp red wine vinegar
- 3 tbsp extra virgin olive oil
- Salt and black pepper

METHOD

1. Cut the skin off the orange using a small knife, making
sure to remove all the white pith, and cut out the orange
segments. Roughly chop the almonds.

2. Warm the Spanish grains according to the packet
instructions. Meanwhile, shake or whisk all the dressing
ingredients together in a jar or bowl.

3. In a large bowl, combine the grains with the orange
segments, rocket, fennel, parsley and almonds. Toss together
with the dressing and arrange on a serving platter or onto
2 plates.

CAJUN LENTILS & KIDNEY BEANS WITH TOMATOES & OLIVE OIL ON TOAST

This is as quick and simple as it gets for a delicious lunch. The warm lentils and garlic toast bring out the best flavour in the tomatoes. If you can't get nice mixed tomatoes, just use good-quality cherry tomatoes.

 SERVES 2   10 MINS

INGREDIENTS

- 1 x 250g pouch of ready cooked Spicy Cajun-Style Lentils & Kidney Beans
- 200g ripe mixed tomatoes, cut into 3cm chunks
- 1 small red onion, very finely diced
- 3 tbsp extra virgin olive oil, plus extra to drizzle
- Juice of ½ lemon
- 2 slices of sourdough bread
- 1 clove of garlic, peeled
- Salt and black pepper

METHOD

1. Microwave the lentils according to the packet instructions, then carefully tip into a large bowl.

2. Add the tomatoes, onion, oil and lemon juice to the bowl and toss together to evenly coat.

3. Toast or griddle the bread slices, then rub the garlic onto the bread – be sparing here as it's very strong when raw.

4. Spoon the tomato and warm lentil mixture onto the toasts, then season with salt and black pepper and drizzle with a little extra oil.

SPEEDY FALAFEL WRAP

This is a cheat's lunch, but it's perfect for when you don't want to deep-fry anything – all the flavour and crunch of a classic falafel but with half the effort and time. The falafel mixture keeps for up to a week in the fridge, and you can shape it into balls and deep-fry into falafels if you want to.

 SERVES 4   20 MINS

INGREDIENTS

For the falafels
- 1 x 250g pouch of ready cooked Beluga® Lentils
- 1 x 400g can chickpeas, drained and rinsed
- 2 cloves of garlic, peeled
- 1 small onion, diced
- Small handful of parsley
- Small handful of coriander
- 1 tsp ground cumin
- 4 tbsp plain flour
- 1 tsp baking powder
- Salt and black pepper
- 3 tbsp olive oil, for frying

To serve
- 200g tub of hummus
- 4 flour tortilla wraps
- ¼ cucumber, peeled into ribbons
- Zest and juice of ½ lemon
- Handful of herbs such as mint, coriander and parsley, leaves picked
- Extra virgin olive oil

METHOD

1. Add all the falafel ingredients except the oil to a food processor and blitz until combined but not totally smooth. The mixture should make a dough that can be formed into a ball and doesn't stick to your hands.

2. Heat the oil in a medium non-stick frying pan over a medium–high heat and, once hot, add single tablespoonfuls of the mixture (about 4 at a time). Lightly pat down with the back of a fork to create a 3cm layer of the mixture. Fry for 3–4 minutes until the underside is golden and crispy.

3. Now flip the falafel over to crisp up the other side – don't worry about keeping it all in one piece as you'll break it up into chunks to serve anyway.

4. Once both sides are crispy and golden, remove from the heat and repeat to cook the remaining falafel mixture.

5. To assemble, add a dollop of hummus to the base of the wrap, top with chunks of the crispy falafel mixture, then the cucumber, lemon zest and juice, herbs, then finally finish with a drizzle of extra virgin olive oil and season with salt and black pepper.

KOREAN GRAIN SALAD BOWL WITH SATAY SAUCE

Smooth and creamy satay dressing and crunchy fresh vegetables make a great combination. You can swap out any of the vegetables for ones you have in the fridge, like red pepper, red or white cabbage, edamame beans or radishes.

 SERVES 2   10 MINS

INGREDIENTS

- 100g mangetout, thinly sliced into strips
- ¼ cucumber, peeled into ribbons
- 1 carrot, peeled into ribbons
- 25g roasted unsalted peanuts, roughly chopped, plus extra to serve
- 1 x 250g pouch of ready cooked Zingy Korean-style Grains

- Juice of ½ lime
- 1 tbsp olive oil
- Small handful of coriander, leaves picked
- Small handful of mint, leaves picked

For the satay sauce
- Zest and juice of ½ lime
- 1 tbsp soy sauce
- 3 tbsp crunchy peanut butter
- 160ml coconut cream

METHOD

1. Add all the sauce ingredients to a blender and blitz until smooth and creamy, adding a little water if you prefer a thinner texture.

2. Toss the vegetables, peanuts and grains together with the lime juice and oil. Transfer to a serving bowl and drizzle over the satay sauce. Scatter with a few extra peanuts and the herbs.

HERBY FATTOUSH WITH GRAINS

In the Middle East, fattoush is a feature of many meals.
Simple to put together and a great way to use up stale bread.

 SERVES 2 ✿ 10 MINS

INGREDIENTS

- 1 x 250g pouch of ready
  cooked Aromatic Persian-
  Style Quinoa & Lentils
- 1 large stale flatbread or pita,
  torn into bite-sized pieces
- 2 medium tomatoes, any
  colour, cut into 2cm chunks
- 50g radishes, thinly sliced
- ½ cucumber, diced
- Small handful of mint, leaves
  chopped
- Small handful of parsley,
  leaves chopped

For the dressing
- 1 clove of garlic, grated or
  finely chopped
- Zest and juice of ½ lemon
- 3 tbsp extra virgin olive oil
- Sea salt flakes and black
  pepper

To serve
- 1 tbsp sumac

METHOD

1. Add all the salad
ingredients to a large
serving or mixing bowl,
squeezing the Persian
grains before opening the
pouch to loosen them.

2. Put all the dressing
ingredients into a bowl
and mix until combined.
Drizzle over the salad,
toss everything together
and serve with a generous
sprinkle of sumac, salt and
black pepper.

CREAMY CASHEW CAESAR SALAD WITH GRATED WALNUTS & PUY LENTILS

If you've got time, soak the cashews for as long as possible – the longer they soak, the creamier they get. It's also worth making extra of this dressing because it's so delicious.

 SERVES 2   50 MINS

INGREDIENTS

- 1 Little Gem lettuce
- 1 x 250g pouch of ready cooked Puy Lentils
- 25g walnuts

For the dressing
- 100g cashew nuts
- 1 clove of garlic, grated
- 1 tbsp capers, plus 1 tbsp to serve
- 1 tbsp nutritional yeast
- 75ml extra virgin olive oil
- Zest and juice of ½ lemon

For the croutons
- 2 tbsp extra virgin olive oil
- Salt and black pepper
- 200g stale sourdough bread

To serve
- 2–3 walnuts

METHOD

1. Start by making the dressing. Soak the cashews in water for 30 minutes while you make the croutons.

2. Combine the oil, salt and black pepper in a bowl, then tear up the bread into 1cm chunks (the rougher the edges of the bread, the better the croutons). Toss the bread in the seasoned oil, making sure every piece is coated in oil. Heat a large non-stick frying pan on a medium heat and fry the croutons until golden all over, turning and tossing every so often.

3. Drain the cashew nuts, reserving 4 tablespoons of the water. Add the nuts to a blender with the remaining dressing ingredients. Blitz until smooth and creamy, gradually adding a little of the cashew water until you get a smooth, silky dressing.

4. Toss the lettuce leaves and lentils with the dressing. Top with the croutons and serve with the extra capers. Finally, grate the walnuts over the top and season with a little salt and black pepper.

ROAST VEGETABLE & MEXICAN GRAIN BOWL

A filling, healthy and quick lunch that's comforting and fresh at the same time. The Mexican grains are the perfect way to get loads of flavour and texture without the fuss of making it all from scratch.

 SERVES 2   35 MINS

INGREDIENTS

- 100g radishes, thinly sliced
- Zest and juice of 1 lime
- 2 large red peppers, deseeded and roughly cut into chunks
- 150g cherry tomatoes on the vine
- 1 red onion, chopped into thin wedges
- 1 courgette, chopped into chunks
- 2 cloves of garlic, kept whole
- 2 tbsp olive oil
- Salt and black pepper
- 1 x 250g pouch of ready cooked Spicy Mexican-Style Grains
- 1 avocado, stoned, peeled and sliced
- Small handful of coriander, leaves picked

METHOD

1. Preheat the oven to 200°C (180°C fan)/Gas mark 6.

2. Put the radishes in a small bowl and squeeze over half the lime juice. Stir so that the radishes turn pink, then set aside.

3. Add the red peppers, cherry tomatoes, onion, courgette and garlic to a roasting tray with the oil and season with salt and black pepper. Roast for 20 minutes until the vegetables are soft and a little caramelised.

4. Remove from the oven and stir in the Mexican grains, then return to the oven for a further 10 minutes.

5. Spoon into bowls and top with the avocado, remaining lime juice, lime zest, coriander and the pickled radishes.

QUINOA, APPLE & HERB SALAD

Salads can have a bad reputation, but this is one exception: crunchy, lemony and filling. Slice all the vegetables (except the apple) at the beginning of the week and place in a ziplock bag or airtight container, giving you the best salad whenever you need it. Simply add the quinoa, apple and dressing when you're ready to eat.

 SERVES 2 10 MINS

INGREDIENTS

- 1 x 250g pouch of ready cooked Red & White Quinoa
- 1 green apple, thinly sliced
- 1 fennel, halved and thinly sliced, fronds kept for garnish
- Small bunch of mint, leaves picked
- Small bunch of parsley, leaves picked
- 100g radishes, thinly sliced
- 1 celery stick, thinly sliced
- 50g almonds, walnuts or hazelnuts, roughly chopped
- ½ red chilli, deseeded and finely chopped (optional)
- Zest and juice of 1 lemon
- 4 tbsp extra virgin olive oil
- Sea salt flakes and black pepper

METHOD

1. Warm the grains according to the packet instructions, then set aside for a minute to cool a little.

2. Add the grains and all the other ingredients to a large mixing bowl and toss together so that everything is evenly coated in the lemon juice and oil. Season with salt and black pepper, garnish with the fennel fronds and serve immediately.

AUBERGINE & LENTIL DIP WITH FLATBREADS

This is the perfect dip to have in the fridge for lunches. If you have a gas hob, you can simply place the aubergines directly on a medium flame and turn every few minutes until charred on the outside and completely soft and collapsed on the inside. This adds a delicious smoky flavour to the aubergines.

 SERVES 2   25 MINS

INGREDIENTS

- 2 large aubergines
- 3 tbsp olive oil
- Salt and black pepper
- Small handful of parsley, finely chopped
- 5 tbsp vegan cream cheese
- 1 x 250g pouch of ready cooked Tomatoey French Puy & Green Lentils
- ½ clove of garlic, grated
- Zest and juice of ½ lemon
- 4–5 tbsp extra virgin olive oil

To serve
- Warm flatbreads

METHOD

1. Preheat the oven to 200°C (180°C fan)/Gas mark 6.

2. Quarter the aubergines lengthways and place them on a roasting tray. Drizzle with the oil and season with salt and black pepper. Rub the oil and seasoning all over the aubergines so that they are evenly coated, then roast for 20 minutes until soft.

3. Remove the aubergines from the oven and allow to cool for a few minutes before spooning out the flesh into a bowl, breaking up any chunky pieces. Add the parsley to the bowl with the cream cheese, lentils, garlic, lemon zest and juice and extra virgin olive oil. Stir well to combine.

4. Season to taste and serve with warm flatbreads.

COCONUT, TURMERIC & WHOLEGRAIN SOUP WITH CRISPY TOFU

The key here is the crispy tofu. Let all the sides get really golden brown before adding to the bowl. This is the best and most delicious quick lunch you can have: creamy, fresh and filling. Spinach or long-stem broccoli would be equally delicious here if you don't have pak choi.

 SERVES 2   25 MINS

INGREDIENTS

- 2 tbsp coconut oil
- 4 spring onions, finely chopped
- 1 clove of garlic, grated
- Handful of coriander, stalks finely chopped and leaves picked
- Thumb-sized piece of ginger, peeled and grated
- 1 tsp ground turmeric
- 1 x 400ml can full-fat coconut milk
- 400ml vegetable stock
- Salt
- 1 x 250g pouch of ready cooked Glorious Grains with Red Rice & Quinoa
- 2 pak choi, halved (quartered if large)
- Juice of 1 lime

For the crispy tofu
- 2 tbsp olive oil
- 250g extra-firm tofu, cut into 3cm cubes

To serve
- 1 tsp chilli oil
- Zest of 1 lime

METHOD

1. Heat the coconut oil in saucepan over a medium–high heat and add the spring onions, garlic, coriander stalks and ginger and fry for 2–3 minutes until soft. Stir in the turmeric for 1 minute until fragrant, then pour in the coconut milk.

2. Fill the empty can of coconut milk with the vegetable stock and give it a swill to release any remaining coconut milk and add it to the pan. Season with salt, then bring to the boil.

3. Reduce the heat to medium and simmer the broth for 10 minutes until it thickens slightly and looks lovely and creamy.

4. Squeeze the pouch of grains slightly to loosen them, then add to the coconut broth along with the pak choi and cook for a further 3 minutes until the ends of the pak choi are tender.

5. For the tofu, heat the oil in a medium frying pan over a medium–high heat and add the tofu. Fry until golden and crispy all over. Remove from the heat and season with salt.

6. Remove the broth from the heat and squeeze in the lime juice. Serve immediately with chunks of crispy tofu, the chilli oil, lime zest and coriander leaves on top.

KOREAN SUMMER ROLLS WITH GINGER & LIME DIPPING SAUCE

A summer classic with no cooking! These rolls are great if you want lunch on the go, and can be made with what you have in the fridge: Little Gem lettuce, radishes, sliced red peppers, red or white cabbage or thinly sliced fennel.

 SERVES 2   30 MINS

INGREDIENTS

- ½ cucumber, cut into thin batons
- 1 carrot, peeled and cut into thin batons
- Small handful of bean sprouts
- Small handful of Thai basil, coriander and mint, leaves picked, plus extra to serve
- 4 spring onions, cut into long, thin strips
- 8 rice-paper wrappers
- 1 x 250g pouch of ready cooked Zingy Korean-style Grains

For the dipping sauce
- 1 clove of garlic, finely grated or chopped
- 2cm piece of ginger, peeled and very finely grated
- ½ red chilli, deseeded and finely chopped
- 1 tbsp caster sugar
- Juice of 2 limes
- 1 tbsp soy sauce

METHOD

1. Get all the vegetables ready along with a shallow bowl of cold water and a large chopping board.

2. Dip the rice paper wrappers one at a time into the water for a few seconds until slightly softened, then carefully place on the chopping board (don't leave the wrappers in the water for too long as they will become too soft and won't roll).

3. Add 2 spoonfuls of the grains along with a small amount of cucumber, carrot, bean sprouts and herbs into the middle of the wrapper, making sure not to overfill as you'll struggle to roll up the wrapper.

4. Fold in the sides of the wrapper, then tightly roll up, tucking everything in as you go. Transfer to a plate and repeat with the other wrappers.

5. To make the dipping sauce, mix all the ingredients together in a small bowl.

6. Serve the rolls with the dipping sauce and extra herbs, if liked.

FENNEL, PEA & COURGETTE SOUP WITH HERBY ITALIAN-STYLE GRAINS

Because of the flavours already in the herby Italian grains pouch, you've got the most delicious soup in minutes. It's an all-year-round dish that can be modified depending on what's in season or what's in the fridge. This would be delicious with leeks, asparagus or spinach. Cosy, fresh and full of goodness. The pesto makes quite a lot but any leftovers will keep in a sealed jar in the fridge for a few days.

 SERVES 2   25 MINS

INGREDIENTS

- 1 tbsp olive oil
- 1 medium onion, finely diced
- 1 medium courgette, diced
- 1 medium fennel, finely diced, fronds kept for garnish
- 1 clove of garlic, finely chopped
- 1L good-quality vegetable stock
- Salt
- 100g frozen peas
- 1 x 250g pouch of ready cooked Herby Italian-Style Grains
- Juice of ½ lemon

For the pesto
- 50g pine nuts
- Large bunch of basil
- 2 tbsp nutritional yeast
- 125ml extra virgin olive oil, plus extra to serve
- 1 small clove of garlic
- Zest and juice of ½ lemon

To serve
- Small handful of basil and parsley leaves, chopped

METHOD

1. Make the pesto by dry-frying the pine nuts for 2–3 minutes. Once cooled, add the pine nuts and the remaining pesto ingredients to a food processor and blitz a few times until combined but not completely smooth.

2. Heat the oil in a medium saucepan on a medium heat, add the onion, courgette and fennel and fry for 5–8 minutes until soft. Add the garlic and fry for 2 more minutes before adding the vegetable stock and a good pinch of salt. Bring to the boil, then reduce to a simmer for 5 minutes, before adding the peas, Italian grains and lemon juice. Cook for a further minute, or until the peas float to the top, then remove from the heat.

3. Spoon the soup into 2 bowls and top with a dollop of pesto, a drizzle of oil and the herbs.

SPICY CAJUN-STYLE LENTIL & KIDNEY BEAN WRAPS

Good food doesn't need to be complicated. The Cajun lentils hold so much flavour that you only need a few fresh bits in the wraps to make the most delicious quick lunch.

 SERVES 2   10 MINS

INGREDIENTS

- 1 x 250g pouch of ready cooked Spicy Cajun-Style Lentils & Kidney Beans
- 2 medium flour tortilla wraps
- 1 carrot, peeled into thin ribbons
- ½ cucumber, peeled into thin ribbons
- 1 avocado, stoned and sliced

For the garlic yogurt
- 3 tbsp vegan Greek-style yogurt
- 1 clove of garlic, finely grated
- Zest and juice of ½ lemon, plus extra juice to serve
- 1 tbsp extra virgin olive oil
- Salt and black pepper

METHOD

1. Heat the lentils and beans according to the packet instructions.

2. For the garlic yogurt, mix all the ingredients together in a small bowl and set aside.

3. To assemble the wraps, spread half the garlic yogurt down the middle of a wrap. Add a few tablespoons of the lentils and beans, followed by half the carrot, cucumber and avocado. Repeat with the other wrap.

4. Season with salt and black pepper and another small squeeze of lemon, then roll up the wraps, slice them in half and serve.

30-Minute Midweek Meals

PERSIAN COURGETTE & SPINACH FRITTERS

This is a great way to use up any left-over, sad-looking herbs in the fridge. If you don't want to deep-fry the fritters, you can just roll them into patties and cook them in a frying pan in a little oil until golden.

 SERVES 4   30 MINS

INGREDIENTS

- 100g spinach, washed
- Small handful of parsley, roughly chopped
- Small handful of basil, roughly chopped
- Small handful of mint, roughly chopped
- 85g sourdough bread blitzed into breadcrumbs, or panko breadcrumbs
- Zest of 1 lemon
- 100g vegan cream cheese
- 1 tbsp plain flour
- 1 x 250g pouch of ready cooked Aromatic Persian-Style Quinoa & Lentils
- 2 medium courgettes, grated
- Salt and black pepper
- 250ml vegetable oil

For the tahini garlic yogurt
- 1 tbsp tahini
- 6 tbsp vegan yogurt
- ½ clove of garlic, very finely chopped or grated
- 2 tbsp best extra virgin olive oil
- Juice of 1 lemon

To serve
- Handful of fresh herbs: dill, parsley, mint, basil, thyme or oregano
- ½ red chilli, very finely chopped

METHOD

1. Heat a large saucepan and cook the spinach for 2–3 minutes until wilted, then tip it into a colander and squeeze out as much excess water as possible.

2. Add the spinach, herbs, breadcrumbs, lemon zest, cream cheese, flour, and quinoa and lentils to a food processor and blend until combined but still with a good amount of texture.

3. In the same colander you used for the spinach, add the courgettes and again, squeeze out as much excess water as you can. Stir the courgettes into the blitzed grain mixture and season with salt and black pepper. The mixture should be thick, so add more flour if you feel you need to.

4. When you're ready to cook, heat the oil in a large high-sided pan over a medium–high heat. Line a tray with kitchen paper.

5. Test if the oil is hot enough by dropping a teaspoon of the mixture into the oil. If it bubbles, you're ready to go (if you have a food thermometer, the oil should be about 180°C).

6. Take a tablespoon of mixture and roughly shape it into an oval fritter between 2 spoons. Add 4 fritters to the oil to prevent overcrowding, and cook for 3–4 minutes until golden and crisp. Remove each fritter from the oil using a slotted spoon and transfer to the prepared tray. Sprinkle with sea salt as soon as you remove them, then repeat with the remaining fritters. Feel free to add more oil if you think it's getting a little low, but remember to wait until it reaches the correct temperature before frying the rest.

7. Make the tahini garlic yogurt by mixing all the ingredients together in a little bowl and season with salt and black pepper. Serve 3–4 fritters per person with a good dollop of the tahini yogurt, and sprinkled with extra herbs and chilli.

MEXICAN CORN SALAD

The Mexican grains contain corn already, but corn works so nicely in salad in our opinion that we like even more of it! The crispy onions take this to another level; we highly recommend making them yourself as they are so easy to prepare. If you have one, use a mandolin to slice the onions for the best results.

 SERVES 2   20 MINS

INGREDIENTS

- 3 corn on the cob, husks removed
- 1 x 250g pouch of ready cooked Spicy Mexican-Style Grains
- Large handful of coriander, chopped
- Salt and black pepper

For the crispy onions
- 4–5 glugs vegetable oil
- 1 onion, halved and very thinly sliced

For the dressing
- Zest and juice of 2 limes
- 1 generous glug of extra virgin olive oil
- ½ tsp harissa

METHOD

1. Start by making the crispy onions. Heat the oil in a medium saucepan and fry the sliced onion over a medium heat for about 7 minutes, stirring occasionally, until golden. Remove with a slotted spoon, drain on kitchen paper and season with salt.

2. Heat a griddle pan to a high heat then, when the pan is piping hot, add the corn cobs and cook, turning every few minutes, until charred all over and cooked through – this should take about 8 minutes. (This works really well on a barbecue too.) Set aside to cool slightly then, using a sharp knife, slice off the kernels into a serving bowl.

3. Heat the grains according to the packet instructions, then add to the bowl with the sweetcorn, along with the chopped coriander.

4. Put all the dressing ingredients in a jam jar, give it a good shake, then pour over the corn. Give everything a good stir, season with salt and black pepper, and serve topped with the crispy onions.

CHUNKY CHARRED COURGETTE & BROCCOLI WITH HERBY ITALIAN-STYLE GRAINS

Broccoli and courgette are often over-cooked, soft and mushy vegetables, but by frying them in a tiny bit of oil like this, they hold their crunch and flavour.

 SERVES 4   15 MINS

INGREDIENTS

- 2 large courgettes, cut into 3cm chunks
- Small head of broccoli, cut into florets
- Zest and juice of 1 lemon
- 2 tbsp olive oil
- 2 sprigs of thyme, leaves picked
- Sea salt flakes and black pepper
- 1 x 250g pouch of ready cooked Herby Italian-Style Grains
- 1 small red chilli, deseeded and finely chopped
- 2 tbsp extra virgin olive oil
- 100g rocket
- Small handful of basil, leaves picked

METHOD

1. Add the courgettes and broccoli to a large bowl and toss with the lemon zest, the olive oil, the thyme and a good pinch of salt and black pepper. Heat a large, dry frying pan over a high heat. Tip in the vegetables and fry for 4–5 minutes on each side until tender and lightly charred.

2. Heat the grains according to the packet instructions.

3. Transfer the vegetables and grains to a bowl, then stir in the lemon juice, chilli, extra virgin olive oil, rocket and basil and season with salt and black pepper. Serve warm or at room temperature.

HUMMUS WITH A QUINOA DUKKAH

This makes a big batch of dukkah, which is so useful to have in the house. Allow the dukkah to cool completely before storing any leftovers in an airtight container. Play around with the spices and nuts you have in the cupboard to make it your own.

 SERVES 2 30 MINS

INGREDIENTS

For the dukkah
- 1 x 250g pouch of ready cooked Red & White Quinoa
- 2 tbsp olive oil
- 20g hazelnuts
- 25g almonds
- 2 tbsp cumin seeds
- 2 tbsp fennel seeds
- 2 tbsp coriander seeds
- 4 tbsp sesame seeds
- 1 tbsp sumac
- Sea salt flakes and black pepper

For the hummus
- 1 x 400g can chickpeas
- Juice of 1 lemon
- 1 clove of garlic, finely chopped
- 2 tbsp tahini
- 2–4 tbsp best extra virgin olive oil, plus extra to drizzle

To serve
- 100g radishes
- Seed & Wholegrain Crackers (see page 98) or flatbreads

METHOD

1. Preheat the oven to 200°C (180°C fan)/Gas mark 6.

2. Spread the quinoa out onto a large roasting tray and drizzle with the oil. Mix well, then roast for 10 minutes until the quinoa starts to dry out and go crisp.

3. Remove from the oven and add the hazelnuts, almonds and spices, then return to the oven for a further 5 minutes until the nuts and spices are toasted and fragrant.

4. Allow to cool in the tray before transferring to a food processor. Pulse a few times to form a rough crumb (this can also be done in batches in a pestle and mortar). Season generously with salt and black pepper.

5. To make the hummus, drain the chickpeas but reserve the liquid in a small jug. Add the chickpeas, lemon juice, garlic, tahini and 3 tablespoons of the chickpea water to a food processor and blend for a few seconds. Add the oil 1 tablespoon at a time until you have a smooth and creamy texture. Season to taste, adding more lemon juice if you think it needs it.

6. Dollop the hummus into a wide bowl and swirl it around using the back of a spoon. Drizzle with a little more oil, then sprinkle with the dukkah and serve with the radishes and crackers or flatbreads for dipping.

POLENTA & BUTTER BEAN MASH WITH GRILLED CABBAGE

Adding butter beans to polenta before blending makes it extra 'buttery' and creamy.

 SERVES 2–3   25 MINS

INGREDIENTS

- 400ml vegetable stock
- 100g simply ground Polenta
- 1 x 400g can butter beans, drained and rinsed
- Sea salt flakes and black pepper
- 4 tbsp extra virgin olive oil
- 2 tbsp olive oil
- 1 large pointed cabbage, cut into quarters lengthways

For the garlic, nut & chilli oil
- 90ml extra virgin olive oil
- 1 red chilli, deseeded and finely sliced
- 5 cloves of garlic, thinly sliced
- 15g almonds, roughly chopped
- 15g hazelnuts, roughly chopped

METHOD

1. Bring the stock to the boil in a medium saucepan, then pour in the polenta in a steady stream, stirring continuously with a wooden spoon or whisk. Stir for 1 minute.

2. Add the butter beans and season generously with salt and black pepper. Remove from the heat and allow to cool for a few minutes, then transfer to a food processor with the extra virgin olive oil and blend until smooth and creamy.

3. Heat a griddle or regular heavy-based frying pan until really hot, then drizzle the olive oil over the cabbage wedges. sprinkle with a little sea salt and rub it all over.

4. Char the wedges cut-side down for 6–8 minutes on both sides until charred and tender at the stem.

5. Meanwhile, make the garlic, nut and chilli oil. Heat the oil in a small saucepan and fry the ingredients for 3–4 minutes over a low heat until the garlic is golden but not burnt.

6. Dollop the warm mash onto a plate and top with the charred cabbage. Pour the garlic, nut and chilli oil all over.

TOMATOEY LENTILS & BEANS ON TOAST

This isn't your usual beans on toast. Tomatoey lentils mixed with soft cannellini beans make for a deliciously comforting mixture, which is great served on crunchy toasted sourdough.

 SERVES 2   10 MINS

INGREDIENTS

- 1 x 250g pouch of ready cooked Tomatoey French Puy & Green Lentils
- 1 x 400g can cannellini beans, drained and rinsed
- 6 Sun-Dried Tomatoes in Sunflower Oil, drained and roughly chopped
- Zest and juice of 1 lemon
- Small handful of parsley, finely chopped
- 4 tbsp best extra virgin olive oil, plus extra for drizzling
- Sea salt flakes and black pepper
- 2 slices of sourdough bread
- 1 clove of garlic

METHOD

1. Heat the lentils and cannellini beans in a small saucepan for 2–3 minutes until hot, then remove from the heat and toss through the sun-dried tomatoes, lemon zest and juice, parsley and oil. Season with salt and black pepper.

2. Heat a griddle pan and char the bread slices on both sides until toasted, then rub the garlic over the toast, drizzling with a little more oil.

3. Pile the lentil and bean mixture on the garlicky toast and serve.

QUICK GREEN GIANT COUSCOUS 'RISOTTO'

Giant couscous makes for a delicious rice alternative, and it's so nutty and much quicker to cook. Use any greens you have lying around to make the green sauce – chard, kale or peas all make great substitutes for the spinach.

 SERVES 4   30 MINS

INGREDIENTS

- 1 tbsp olive oil
- 1 onion, finely chopped
- 1 celery stick, finely chopped
- 1 clove of garlic, finely chopped
- 200g dried Wholewheat Giant Couscous
- 100ml white wine
- 500–600ml hot vegetable stock

For the green sauce
- 100g spinach
- Handful of basil, plus extra to serve
- Handful of parsley
- Juice of 1 lemon
- 3 tbsp extra virgin olive oil, plus extra to serve

To serve
- 30g vegan parmesan
- Sea salt flakes and black pepper

METHOD

1. Start by making the green sauce. Put the spinach, basil, parsley and lemon juice in a blender with the oil and blitz until smooth and bright green.

2. Heat the oil in a large saucepan over a medium–high heat and fry the onion and celery for 5 minutes until soft. Stir in the garlic and couscous and cook for a further 3–4 minutes. Pour in the white wine and stir again.

3. Once the wine is absorbed, add the vegetable stock, little by little, stirring with each addition and cooking for 12–16 minutes until the couscous is tender, adding more stock if needed.

4. Stir the green sauce into the couscous. Turn off the heat and allow the 'risotto' to sit for a minute or so.

5. Serve with a grating of vegan parmesan, basil leaves, a drizzle of oil, and season with salt and black pepper.

KIMCHI FRIED ZINGY KOREAN-STYLE GRAINS

Kimchi is fermented vegetables in chilli, ginger and garlic and it's a plant-based gem! Just check the ingredients on the jar, as it can occasionally be made with fish sauce.

 SERVES 2   15 MINS

INGREDIENTS

- 1 tbsp olive oil
- Bunch of spring onions, finely chopped
- 1 clove of garlic, finely chopped
- Handful of coriander, leaves picked and stems finely chopped
- Thumb-sized piece of ginger, peeled and finely chopped
- Sea salt flakes and black pepper
- 3 tbsp of good-quality kimchi
- 250g Brussels sprouts, spring greens, chard or Chinese cabbage, shredded
- 1 x 250g pouch of ready cooked Zingy Korean-style Grains
- Zest and juice of ½ lime
- 2 tsp soy sauce
- 2 tsp sesame seeds

METHOD

1. Heat the oil in a large non-stick frying pan over a medium–high heat and fry the spring onions, garlic, coriander stalks and ginger with a pinch of salt.

2. Add the kimchi and fry for a few minutes, then add your chosen greens, stirring for a few more minutes before adding the grains. Cook for 5–6 minutes until the grains start to crisp up a little.

3. Add the lime juice and soy sauce and season with salt and black pepper.

4. Serve with the coriander leaves, sesame seeds and lime zest sprinkled over the top.

CAJUN FLATBREADS

It takes just 20 minutes to get this tastiest of dinners on the table!

 SERVES 2   20 MINS

INGREDIENTS

- 2 tbsp olive oil
- 2 onions, finely chopped
- 2 jarred red peppers, roughly chopped
- Sea salt flakes and black pepper
- 1 x 250g pouch of ready cooked Spicy Cajun-Style Lentils & Kidney Beans
- 1 x 400g can chopped tomatoes
- 1 tbsp tomato purée
- 2 flatbreads (for homemade, see page 112)
- Small handful of oregano, leaves picked
- Small handful of mint, leaves picked

For the garlic yogurt
- 4 tbsp vegan Greek-style yogurt
- ½ clove of garlic, grated or very finely chopped
- 2 tbsp extra virgin olive oil

METHOD

1. Heat the oil in a large non-stick frying pan over a medium–high heat and fry the onions and red peppers with a pinch of salt for 4–5 minutes until the onions are soft.

2. Stir in the lentils, tomatoes and tomato purée, then simmer for about 10 minutes, stirring occasionally until reduced.

3. Meanwhile, make the garlic yogurt by mixing all the ingredients in a small bowl.

4. Warm the flatbreads in a toaster or directly over a low gas flame, if you have one, for a lovely charred effect. Top the flatbreads with the tomatoey mixture and finish with the garlic yogurt, herbs and a bit more seasoning.

QUINOA & ONION BHAJIS

The quinoa is the key element here (as well as the onions of course) because they make the edges of the bhaji crispy and crunchy – like pockets of texture around the onions. For a bigger meal, serve with a curry from page 68 or 121.

 MAKES 12 (SERVES 4)   **30 MINS**

INGREDIENTS

- 2 onions, very finely sliced
- 100g plain flour
- ½ tsp baking powder
- 1 small green chilli, deseeded and finely chopped
- Handful of coriander, stalks finely chopped
- ½ tsp ground turmeric
- ½ tsp ground cumin
- ½ tsp garam masala
- ½ tsp sea salt
- 1 x 250g pouch of ready cooked Red & White Quinoa
- 300ml vegetable oil, for frying

For the green chutney
- 5 tbsp coconut yogurt
- 1 small green chilli, deseeded and finely chopped
- Zest and juice of ½ lemon
- 2 tbsp olive oil
- Large handful of coriander leaves
- Small handful of mint leaves
- Sea salt

METHOD

1. Soak the onion slices in a bowl of water for 10 minutes. In a separate mixing bowl, mix the flour, baking powder, chilli, coriander stalks, spices and salt until combined, then slowly add about 100ml cold water to form a thick batter.

2. To make the green chutney, add all the ingredients to a blender, reserving a few mint and coriander leaves for serving. Blitz everything together until you have a smooth sauce, season to taste, adding more lemon, oil or salt if it needs it. Pour into a small bowl and set aside for serving.

3. Drain the onion from the water and mix it into the spiced batter. Squeeze the pouch slightly to loosen the quinoa, then add this to the onions. Give everything a good stir until the onion slices and quinoa are evenly coated in the batter.

4. Heat the vegetable oil in a medium, high-sided, heavy-based saucepan until it reaches about 180°C. If you don't have a food thermometer, just drop a little of the mixture into the oil and if it sizzles, you're ready to go. Be careful not to overheat the oil: you want the bhajis to be golden outside with a soft centre; if the oil is too hot, you'll burn the outside and the centre will remain raw and doughy.

5. Line a plate or tray with kitchen paper ready to drain the bhajis. Spoon heaped tablespoons of the bhaji mixture into the oil, making sure you don't cook more than 3 at a time and overcrowd the pan. Cook for 3–4 minutes, turning once or twice until evenly golden and crisp. Remove with a slotted spoon and drain on the kitchen paper. Sprinkle with salt while still hot and repeat with the remaining mixture.

6. Serve with the green chutney and reserved herbs.

CRISPY GINGER, GARLIC & MAPLE LENTILS WITH NOODLES, RADISHES & VIETNAMESE DRESSING

Crisping up the lentils like this is so moreish, especially when served with silky noodles and lime dressing. It's a weekly go-to and can be served with any crunchy veg in your fridge, like bean sprouts, mangetout, peppers, carrots etc.

 SERVES 2   15 MINS

INGREDIENTS

- 1 tbsp sesame oil
- 5cm piece of ginger, peeled and grated
- 1 clove of garlic, finely chopped or grated
- 3 spring onions, finely chopped
- 200g chestnut mushrooms, diced
- 1 x 250g pouch of ready cooked Puy Lentils
- 1 tsp maple syrup
- Sea salt flakes
- 150g brown rice noodles

Lime dressing
- Zest and juice of 1 lime
- 2cm piece of ginger, peeled and finely grated
- 1 tsp soy sauce
- 1 tbsp sesame oil

To serve
- 50g radishes, thinly sliced
- 2 spring onions, thinly sliced
- Small handful of coriander, leaves pickled
- Small handful of mint, leaves pickled

METHOD

1. Start by making the lentils. Heat the oil in a non-stick frying pan over a medium–high heat and fry the ginger, garlic, spring onions, mushrooms and lentils for 5–8 minutes until the mushrooms release their liquid and start to crisp up and caramelise. Add the maple syrup, stirring immediately so it doesn't burn, then turn off the heat and season with salt.

2. Cook the noodles according to the packet instructions, drain and set aside.

3. While the noodles and lentils are cooking, prepare the dressing. Add all the ingredients to a jar or small bowl and whisk together.

4. Serve in a bowl with a pile of noodles, the crispy lentils, radishes, spring onions and herbs. Drizzle over the dressing.

Easy
Plant-Based
Classics

QUINOA VEGGIE BALLS IN A SLOW-COOKED CHERRY TOMATO & CAPER SAUCE

The cherry tomatoes make this sauce so delicious and silky. It makes for a great all-rounder sauce too, so if you're in the mood, make double for pasta or pizza later in the week.

 SERVES 4 1 HR 15 MINS

INGREDIENTS

- 5 tbsp olive oil
- 1 small red onion, finely chopped
- 2 cloves of garlic, finely chopped
- ½ tsp smoked paprika
- 2 sprigs of rosemary, leaves roughly chopped
- 1 x 400g can black beans, drained and rinsed
- 1 x 250g pouch of ready cooked Red & White Quinoa
- Small handful of parsley, roughly chopped
- 2 tbsp plain flour
- 2 tbsp tomato purée
- Salt and black pepper

For the tomato sauce
- 5 tbsp extra virgin olive oil
- 750g cherry tomatoes
- 2 cloves of garlic, finely chopped
- Handful of capers
- Handful of basil leaves

To serve
- Extra virgin olive oil
- Small handful of basil, leaves picked
- Fresh bread
- Salad and/or any vegan pasta

METHOD

1. Heat 2 tablespoons of the oil in a frying pan and fry the onion on a medium heat for 4–6 minutes until soft. Add the garlic and fry for a further 2 minutes before adding the paprika and rosemary.

2. In a food processor add the black beans, quinoa, parsley, flour, tomato purée and onion mixture and blitz a few times until you have a rough dough that doesn't stick to your hands. You can add a little more flour if you feel like it needs it. Season with salt and black pepper.

3. Roll the mixture into 16 even-sized balls, then place on a tray or plate and chill in the fridge for 30 minutes, or overnight.

4. Preheat the oven to 200°C (180°C fan)/Gas mark 6.

Continued...

5. Now make the tomato sauce. In the same pan as you cooked the onion, heat 2 tablespoons of the oil over a low–medium heat and add the cherry tomatoes and garlic. Cook for 30 minutes, bursting the tomatoes as they cook to create a sauce. Keep an eye on the heat as you don't want the garlic to burn, so make sure the sauce is simmering very gently. Once you have a rich, sticky sauce, stir in the remaining 3 tablespoons of olive oil, the capers and basil. Season with salt and black pepper and set aside.

6. In a separate frying pan, heat the remaining 3 tablespoons olive oil on a medium–high heat and add the quinoa balls. Fry for a few minutes until crispy all over. You might have to do this in batches, so just fry off and add to a baking tray as you go.

7. Pop the crispy quinoa balls into the oven to cook through for 15–20 minutes before dropping them into the tomato sauce.

8. Serve with a drizzle of extra virgin olive oil, fresh basil, bread and a salad or vegan pasta.

LENTIL DHAL TOPPED WITH ROAST BEETROOT & CHUNKY COCONUT RAITA

If you haven't got time to pre-roast the beetroot from raw, pre-cooked beetroot works just as well. You can also swap the beetroot for cauliflower, carrots, tomatoes, pumpkin or sweet potato, so use what you have in the fridge or what's in season.

 SERVES 4    1 HR 40 MINS

INGREDIENTS

- 1 tsp cumin seeds
- 1 tsp mustard seeds
- 2 tbsp olive oil
- 3 large onions, very thinly sliced
- 3 cloves of garlic, chopped
- Large thumb-sized piece of ginger, peeled and grated or finely chopped
- 1 tsp ground turmeric
- 1 tsp ground coriander
- 1 tsp chilli flakes (optional)
- 4 large tomatoes, cut into small pieces
- 200g dried Puy lentils
- 1 x 400ml can full-fat coconut milk
- 400ml vegetable stock
- Juice of ½ lemon
- Salt and black pepper

For the roast beetroot
- 3 medium beetroot
- 5 cloves of garlic, left whole
- 3 tbsp olive oil
- 1 tsp cumin seeds
- 1 tsp mustard seeds

For the raita
- 4 tbsp coconut yogurt
- ½ cucumber, cut into small chunks
- Small handful of mint leaves, chopped
- Small handful of coriander leaves, chopped
- 2 tbsp desiccated coconut
- Olive oil

To serve
- Mango chutney
- Small handful of coriander leaves
- Nigella seeds
- Chapati, naan bread and/or flatbread

METHOD

1. Preheat the oven to 220°C (200°C fan)/Gas mark 7.

2. Start by roasting the beetroot. Wrap each beetroot in foil then place in a roasting tray and roast for 40–50 minutes, or until soft. Remove the foil and allow the beetroot to cool slightly before peeling off the skins. Chop into large chunks, then return to the roasting tray with the garlic, oil, cumin and mustard seeds and roast for a further 25 minutes.

Continued...

3. Meanwhile, dry-fry the cumin and mustard seeds in a frying pan over a medium heat for 1–2 minutes until fragrant. Remove from the heat and crush in a pestle and mortar (this can also be done on a chopping board, crushing with the flat side of a knife).

4. In the same pan, heat the oil, add the onions, seasoning with salt, and slowly sweat on a medium heat for 10–15 minutes, making sure the onions are really soft. Increase the heat a little and add the garlic and ginger and fry for a few more minutes before adding all the spices, including the crushed mustard and cumin seeds. Stir everything together to allow the spices to get lovely and fragrant, then add the tomatoes, lentils, coconut milk and vegetable stock.

5. Bring to a boil, then simmer over a very low heat for 30 minutes until the lentils are cooked and the dhal is creamy. Stir every 10–15 minutes, ensuring the mixture doesn't stick to the bottom of the pan, adding a splash of water or stock if it feels like it's drying out.

6. Mix all the raita ingredients together in a bowl, season with salt and pepper and set aside.

7. Once everything is ready, squeeze the lemon juice into the dhal and serve with a spoonful of the roasted beetroot, a good dollop of raita, some mango chutney, coriander leaves and nigella seeds. Mop it all up with a selection of Indian breads.

LENTIL, SPINACH, MUSHROOM & POTATO PIE

This recipe is simple but so comforting. It makes a proper winter dinner with minimal effort. A good tip here is to make sure the mushrooms are really golden and caramelised before adding the other ingredients as they hold the key to a really tasty pie.

 SERVES 4   1 HR

INGREDIENTS

- 2 tbsp olive oil, plus extra for brushing
- 3 shallots, finely chopped
- 500g mushrooms (a mixture of chestnut, shiitake, girolle or portobello), halved or quartered
- 2 cloves of garlic, finely chopped
- 4 sprigs of thyme, leaves picked, plus extra to sprinkle
- 1 x 250g pouch of ready cooked Beluga® Lentils
- 1 tbsp plain flour
- 150ml vegetable stock
- 100ml oat cream
- Large handful of parsley, finely chopped
- 500g spinach, washed
- Salt and black pepper
- 3 medium potatoes

METHOD

1. Heat the oil in a large frying pan over a medium heat, then add the shallots and a pinch of salt and fry for 2–3 minutes. Add the mushrooms and fry for 6–8 minutes so they release their liquid and start to caramelise.

2. Add in the garlic and thyme and cook for another few minutes before adding the lentils.

3. Add the flour, stirring for a few minutes to cook out, then slowly pour in the vegetable stock followed by the oat cream and parsley. Bring to a boil, then reduce the heat to a simmer for a few minutes until the mixture is thick and creamy. Add the spinach and stir until wilted, season with salt and black pepper, then remove from the heat and pour the mixture into a medium baking dish.

4. Preheat the oven to 200°C (180°C fan)/Gas mark 6.

5. Peel and slice the potatoes into 1mm thick slices (or as thin as you can go), then arrange them in a neat spiral on top of the mushroom filling so that the whole top is covered.

6. Season with salt and black pepper and sprinkle with a little extra thyme. Bake for 25–30 minutes until golden and bubbling.

WHOLE CHESTNUT, SPINACH, SQUASH & ONION FILO TART

This is based very loosely on a Greek spanakopita but of course, without the feta. When roasting the squash, make sure it's got a good caramelisation on all sides before removing from the oven. This will ensure a delicious sweet flavour.

 SERVES 4   1 HR 10 MINS

INGREDIENTS

- 800g–1kg butternut squash, peeled, deseeded and cut into 2cm cubes
- 3 cloves of garlic, kept whole and skin on
- 1 onion, halved and sliced into thin wedges
- 1 tsp fresh or dried oregano
- 5 tbsp extra virgin olive oil, plus extra for greasing
- 1 tsp flaked sea salt
- Black pepper
- 500g spinach, tough stalks removed
- Zest of 1 lemon
- 1 x 180g pouch of ready cooked Whole Chestnuts, halved
- 100g pine nuts
- 40g dried breadcrumbs
- Small handful of parsley, chopped
- 6 sheets of filo pastry, each around 48 x 25cm

METHOD

1. Preheat the oven to 220°C (200°C fan)/Gas mark 7.

2. Add the butternut squash, garlic, onion and oregano to a large roasting tray and drizzle with 2 tablespoons of the oil, the salt and some black pepper. Toss together, then roast for 25 minutes until everything is slightly caramelised and soft.

3. Add the spinach to a large saucepan and cook in batches (a couple of handfuls at a time) for about 3 minutes, or until the spinach is very soft, stirring constantly. Drain the spinach through a sieve, pressing with the back of a spoon to remove as much liquid as possible. Leave everything to cool for about 15–20 minutes.

4. Squeeze the garlic out its papery case and squish it slightly with the back of a knife. Add the garlic, squash mixture, spinach, lemon zest, chestnuts, pine nuts, breadcrumbs and parsley to a mixing bowl and combine, mashing some of the squash but keeping a few pieces whole.

5. Grease the base and sides of a 20cm round loose-bottomed cake tin with a little oil. Lay a sheet of filo pastry in the tin, making sure you have an even overhang all round. Brush all over with oil and repeat with another sheet of filo, working clockwise so that you end up with full and even layering covering all sides of the tin. Repeat with 3 more sheets of filo, brushing with oil before adding the next layer.

6. Add the filling to the tin, then fold over the overhanging filo into the centre. Brush the remaining sheet of filo with oil, then scrunch it up and place it on top to form a messy crust. Brush again with oil, season with salt, then bake for 25–30 minutes until golden brown and crisp.

SQUASH CURRY WITH GLORIOUS GRAINS

This packs all the flavours of a tikka masala. The hidden but very important ingredient is the ground almonds, so whatever you do, don't forget to add them. This is even more delicious the day after, so we recommend making the sauce the day before or just save half for leftovers.

 SERVES 4   1 HR 10 MINS

INGREDIENTS

For the roast squash
- 1 large squash (weighing about 1kg)
- 1 tbsp extra virgin olive oil
- 1 tbsp garam masala
- Sea salt

For the sauce
- 1 tsp coriander seeds
- 1 tsp cumin seeds
- 1 tsp ground coriander
- 1 tsp sweet smoked paprika
- 1 tsp ground turmeric
- 2 tbsp olive oil
- 2 onions, finely chopped
- 3 cloves of garlic, finely chopped
- Thumb-sized piece of ginger, peeled and grated or finely chopped
- ½ red chilli, deseeded and chopped
- 150g cherry tomatoes
- 2 tbsp tomato purée
- 1 x 400ml can full-fat coconut milk
- 20g ground almonds

To serve
- 1 x 250g pouch of ready cooked Glorious Grains with Red Rice & Quinoa
- 50g almonds, roughly chopped
- Poppadoms or naan bread
- Coconut yogurt
- Mango chutney

METHOD

1. Preheat the oven to 220°C (200°C fan)/Gas mark 7.

2. Halve the squash and deseed it, then cut it into 3cm chunks (we like to keep the skin on for flavour, but feel free to peel if you want). Add to a large roasting tray with the oil, garam masala and a pinch of salt. Toss, then spread out in a single layer and roast for 30 minutes until golden and soft.

3. Meanwhile make the sauce. Heat a deep frying pan or pot over a medium-high heat and dry-fry the spices for 2 minutes until they start to smell fragrant. Tip into a pestle and mortar and crush to a coarse powder.

Continued...

4. In the same pan, heat the oil over a medium heat and fry the onions for 8–10 minutes until really soft and caramelised. Add the garlic, ginger and chilli to the pan and cook on a gentle heat for a further 2–3 minutes.

5. Add the spices to the onion pan, then stir in the tomatoes and tomato purée and cook for 2–3 minutes. Stir in the coconut milk and ground almonds, bring to a gentle simmer over a low heat and bubble, uncovered, for 15 minutes, stirring to stop the sauce from sticking to the bottom of the pan. To finish, stir in the roasted squash.

6. Heat the grains according to the packet instructions, then transfer to a serving bowl while hot and steaming.

7. Serve the curry in a large dish in the middle of the table with the almonds sprinkled on top and the grains, poppadoms or naan bread, coconut yogurt and mango chutney on the side.

A TWIST ON MOUSSAKA, WITH COURGETTES & LENTILS

This is a moussaka-inspired recipe, but with charred and tender courgettes instead of aubergines. It is certainly not traditional, but there are no compromises on flavour. It has a few different elements, but each very quick and simple to pull together, so don't be deterred by the ingredients list.

 SERVES 4   50 MINS

INGREDIENTS

- 4 courgettes, sliced into 1cm strips lengthways
- 2 tbsp olive oil
- Salt and black pepper
- Zest and juice of 1 lemon
- Handful of parsley, roughly chopped
- Small handful of oregano, leaves picked

For the lentil base
- 2 tbsp olive oil
- 1 large onion, finely chopped
- 2 cloves of garlic, finely chopped
- 1 tsp paprika
- 1 tsp dried oregano or small bunch of fresh, leaves picked
- ½ tsp ground cinnamon
- 1 x 400g can chopped tomatoes
- 1 x 250g pouch of ready cooked Tomatoey French Puy & Green Lentils

For the béchamel sauce
- 4 tbsp vegan butter
- 4 tbsp plain flour
- 800ml oat milk (or any vegan milk you prefer)
- 3 tbsp nutritional yeast
- Small grating of nutmeg

For the breadcrumb topping
- 4 tbsp olive oil
- 100g breadcrumbs

To serve
- Vegan feta (optional)

METHOD

1. Preheat the oven to 120°C (100°C fan)/Gas mark ½.

2. Start by making the lentil base. Heat the oil in a saucepan over a medium–high heat and fry the onion for 4–6 minutes until soft. Add the garlic and cook for a further 2 minutes, then add the paprika, oregano and cinnamon.

3. Pour in the tomatoes and lentils, bring to a boil, then simmer for 20 minutes, stirring occasionally until thickened.

4. Meanwhile, add the courgettes to a mixing bowl and pour over the olive oil, season with salt and black pepper, then toss together so all the slices are evenly coated.

Continued...

5. Heat a griddle pan until piping hot, then lay the courgette slices on and cook for 2–4 minutes on each side, in batches, until charred and soft. Once cooked, add to a roasting tray and place in the oven to keep warm while you do the rest.

6. To make the béchamel sauce, melt the vegan butter in a saucepan over a medium heat. Add the flour and stir to form a loose paste. Cook for 1–2 minutes, then add a little milk and stir again.

7. Keep adding the milk gradually so that it forms a thick paste, then add more and more until you have a smooth, creamy sauce. Add the nutritional yeast, nutmeg and season with salt and pepper, then remove from the heat.

8. Now prepare the breadcrumb topping. Heat the oil in a small frying pan over a medium–high heat and fry the breadcrumbs until golden.

9. Remove the courgettes from the oven, squeeze over the lemon juice, and sprinkle with the zest and herbs. Season with salt and black pepper.

10. Serve the griddled courgettes on a large serving platter with the lentil ragu and béchamel sauce in separate bowls or straight from the pans so that everyone can assemble their own bowl, topped with crunchy breadcrumbs.

TRIPLE TOMATO LENTIL RAGU WITH TAGLIATELLE

It might seem mad to use three different types of tomato for this sauce, but they all bring a completely different flavour. The roast tomatoes are sweet and soft, the canned tomatoes provide the base, and the sun-dried tomatoes and nutty lentils add the final richness.

 SERVES 4 1 HR 10 MINS

INGREDIENTS

- 700g cherry or medium tomatoes on the vine
- 4 cloves of garlic, peeled but left whole
- 6 tbsp olive oil
- 2 tsp dried oregano
- Salt and black pepper
- 2 celery sticks, finely chopped
- 1 shallot, finely chopped
- 2 sprigs of rosemary, leaves finely chopped
- 1 x 250g pouch of ready cooked Beluga® Lentils
- 1 x 400g can chopped tomatoes
- 6 Sun-Dried Tomatoes in Sunflower Oil, drained and roughly chopped

To serve
- 250g vegan tagliatelle or spaghetti
- Fresh basil leaves
- Extra virgin olive oil
- Vegan parmesan (optional)

METHOD

1. Preheat the oven to 200°C (180°C fan)/Gas mark 6.

2. Add the fresh tomatoes and garlic to a large roasting tray, pour over 4 tablespoons of the oil and add the oregano. Season with salt and black pepper, toss and roast for 30–35 minutes.

3. While the tomatoes are roasting, heat the remaining 2 tablespoons of oil in a large saucepan over a medium heat and add the celery, shallot and rosemary with a pinch of salt. Gently fry on a medium heat for 5 minutes until everything is soft.

4. Remove and discard the vines from the tomatoes, then stir into the onion mixture, along with the lentils, canned tomatoes, and sun-dried tomatoes. Bring to a boil, then simmer for 20 minutes, stirring occasionally so that the bottom doesn't catch, until reduced to a thick, silky sauce.

5. Boil the tagliatelle according to the packet instructions, then drain, saving a mugful of the pasta water.

6. Stir the sauce into the pasta, adding a little of the pasta water so it's lovely and silky. Serve in bowls, topped with a few basil leaves, a drizzle of oil and a grating of vegan parmesan, if liked.

LENTIL CHILI 'NON' CARNE WITH EXTRA-CRISPY CUMIN JACKET POTATOES

Nothing says 'cosy' like a jacket potato and chili. By rubbing the potatoes in oil and seasoning with salt and cumin, the skins become amazingly crispy. Freestyle with the toppings – a dollop of vegan yogurt or soured cream is a great addition.

 SERVES 4    1 HR 30 MINS

INGREDIENTS

- 2 tbsp olive oil
- 2 medium onions, diced
- 2 celery sticks, diced
- 1 red pepper, diced
- 4 cloves of garlic, grated
- ¼ tsp chilli powder
- 2 tsp ground cumin
- 2 tsp ground coriander
- 1 tsp smoked paprika
- 2 tsp dried oregano
- 2 tbsp tomato purée
- 5 Sun-Dried Tomatoes in Sunflower Oil, sliced
- 2 x 400g cans chopped tomatoes
- 1 x 400g can chickpeas
- 1 x 400g can red kidney beans
- 1 x 250g pouch of ready cooked Tomatoey French Puy & Green Lentils

For the jacket potatoes
- 4 large floury potatoes
- 1 tbsp olive oil
- 2 tsp cumin seeds
- Salt flakes and black pepper

To serve
- 2 avocados, peeled and diced
- Handful of coriander leaves
- Zest and juice of 2 limes

METHOD

1. Preheat the oven to 200°C (180°C fan)/Gas mark 6.

2. Start with the jacket potatoes. Lay them out on a baking tray and drizzle over the oil, sprinkle with the cumin seeds and season with salt and black pepper. Using your hands, rub the oil and seasoning all over the potatoes, then prick them a few times and place in the oven for 1–1½ hours, depending on the size of the potatoes. They should be crispy and golden on the outside and fluffy in the middle.

3. Heat the oil in a large, heavy-based saucepan over a medium heat and cook the onions, celery and red pepper for about 5 minutes, or until really soft. Add the garlic and cook for a further 2 minutes before adding the spices and oregano. Fry for 1–2 minutes until fragrant.

4. Stir in the tomato purée, sun-dried tomatoes and canned tomatoes. Bring to a boil, then reduce the heat and simmer for 10 minutes. Drain and rinse the chickpeas and kidney beans. Add them and the lentils to the pan and simmer for a further 20–30 minutes, stirring regularly. Season generously, then turn off the heat once you're happy with the consistency.

5. Remove the potatoes from the oven and slice them open. Dollop a good pile of the chili in the middle and serve with avocado, coriander, lime zest and a squeeze of lime juice.

Optional extra: for pickled onions, halve then thinly slice 1 medium red onion and put in a bowl with the juice from ½ lemon. Rub the juice into the onions until the juice turns pink and set aside to pickle until you're ready to serve.

PUY LENTIL RAGU LASAGNE

The lentils add a nutty, rich flavour and meaty texture to the base of this lasagne. Make double the ragu so you can either freeze it for another day or add it to pasta later in the week.

 SERVES 6   1 HR 40 MINS

INGREDIENTS

- 2 tbsp olive oil
- 2 onions, diced
- 1 celery stick, finely diced
- 200g chestnut mushrooms, finely chopped
- 2 cloves of garlic, finely chopped
- 2 sprigs of rosemary, leaves chopped
- 200g dried Puy lentils
- 2 tbsp tomato purée
- 4 Sun-Dried Tomatoes in Sunflower Oil, drained and finely chopped
- 1 x 400g can chopped tomatoes
- 400ml vegetable stock or water
- 9–10 dried lasagne sheets (ensure they are egg-free)
- 100g breadcrumbs
- Extra virgin olive oil, to drizzle

For the béchamel sauce
- 4 tbsp vegan butter
- 4 tbsp plain flour
- 800ml oat milk (or any vegan milk you prefer)
- 3 tbsp nutritional yeast
- Salt and black pepper

METHOD

1. Preheat the oven to 200°C (180°C fan)/Gas mark 6.

2. Heat the oil in a large, heavy-based saucepan over a medium heat and cook the onions, celery and mushrooms for about 8 minutes, or until the onion is soft and the mushrooms are golden. Add the garlic and rosemary and continue cooking for 2 minutes. Stir in the lentils, tomato purée, sun-dried tomatoes, canned tomatoes and stock, then bring to the boil. Reduce the heat and simmer for 30–35 minutes until the lentils are soft and the sauce has thickened.

3. To make the béchamel sauce, melt the butter in a saucepan over a medium heat. Add the flour and stir, using a wooden spoon, to form a loose paste. Cook for 1–2 minutes, then add a little milk and stir again. Keep adding the milk slowly and gradually to form a thick paste, then add more until you have a smooth, creamy sauce. Add the nutritional yeast and season with salt and pepper, then remove from the heat.

4. Spoon a few tablespoons of the ragu into a deep, 30 x 20cm ovenproof dish. Spread it out evenly, then place a single layer of pasta sheets on top, breaking some up so you have total coverage.

5. Spoon over a generous layer of béchamel sauce, then repeat until the sauce is used up and you finish with a layer of the béchamel sauce.

6. Sprinkle over the breadcrumbs, season with salt and black pepper, then drizzle with a little oil and bake for 35 minutes until golden and bubbling.

BELUGA LENTIL, ROASTED PEPPER, TOMATO & AUBERGINE MIX

This is a real crowd pleaser and one you'll make time and time again. The aubergine, tomato, pepper and onion mixture can be tossed into any warmed grain, but the Beluga® lentils are particularly delicious.

 SERVES 4   45 MINS

INGREDIENTS

- 4 aubergines, halved lengthways
- 1 onion, cut into thin wedges
- 2 red romano peppers, halved lengthways and deseeded
- 400g cherry tomatoes
- 3 cloves of garlic, left whole in their skins
- 2 tbsp olive oil
- Salt and black pepper
- 1 x 250g pouch of ready cooked Beluga® Lentils
- Zest and juice of 1 lemon

To serve
- Small handful of parsley, leaves picked
- Small handful of oregano, leaves picked
- Extra virgin olive oil
- Crusty bread

METHOD

1. Preheat the oven to 220°C (200°C fan)/Gas mark 7.

2. Put the aubergines, onion, red peppers, tomatoes and garlic in a large roasting tray. Drizzle with the oil and season with salt and black pepper. Roast for 30–35 minutes until the aubergines, onion and tomatoes are blistered and soft, then remove from the oven and set aside to cool a little.

3. Scoop out the flesh of the aubergines, peel off the skin of the peppers and squeeze out the garlic from their papery skins. Squash the garlic a little, then add all these to a bowl with the lentils, tomatoes, onion, lemon zest and juice. Season with salt and black pepper.

4. Toss everything together and serve on a large platter with the fresh herbs, a little more oil and some bread.

SPICED SWEET POTATO, GRAIN & RED ONION EMPANADAS

This is a sort of burrito and empanada hybrid – perfect for a picnic
or lunch on the go. With the clever little Mexican grain pouch,
you've got so much flavour with little effort.

 MAKES 8 (SERVES 4)   1 HR 15 MINS

INGREDIENTS

- 550g sweet potatoes, peeled and cut into 2–3cm cubes
- 1 red onion, cut into thin wedges
- 2 tbsp olive oil
- 1 tsp paprika
- 1 tsp ground cumin
- 1 tsp ground coriander
- Salt and black pepper
- 1 x 250g pouch of ready cooked Spicy Mexican-Style Grains
- Small handful of fresh coriander, roughly chopped
- Zest and juice of 1 lime
- 2 tbsp nut milk
- Pinch of sugar
- 2 x 320g vegan ready-rolled puff pastry sheets
- Flour, for dusting (optional)

METHOD

1. Preheat the oven to 220°C (200°C fan)/Gas mark 7.

2. Add the sweet potatoes and onion to a large roasting tray with the oil, paprika, cumin and ground coriander and toss to coat the potatoes and onion in the spices. Season with salt and black pepper. Roast for 25–30 minutes until soft and slightly caramelised. Remove from the oven and set aside to cool. Reduce the oven temperature to 200°C (180°C fan)/Gas mark 6.

3. Add the sweet potatoes and onion to a bowl with the grains, fresh coriander, lime zest and juice, and season with salt and black pepper. Mix together, mashing a few bits of sweet potato as you go.

4. In a small bowl, mix the milk with the sugar (adding sugar to the milk will give the glaze a lovely gloss). Place the pastry sheets onto a floured surface or baking paper, then cut out eight 12cm discs using either a cutter or a small bowl. Place a heaped tablespoon of filling in the centre of a disc. Brush half the edge of pastry with a little milk, then fold the other half over. Crimp the edges using either a fork of your fingers to seal, then lay out on a large baking tray. Repeat to fill and seal the remaining pastry discs.

5. Brush the tops with the remaining milk, then bake for 25–30 minutes until golden brown. Leave to cool for a few minutes before serving.

SMOKY SPANISH WHOLEGRAIN PAELLA

If you want to make this dish a bit heartier, add some halved, jarred artichokes to the pan with the peppers at the start. They make a really good addition, but they can be on the expensive side, so this is optional.

 SERVES 4   20 MINS

INGREDIENTS

- Small pinch of saffron
- 150ml hot vegetable stock
- 2 tbsp olive oil
- 1 large onion, finely chopped
- 2 red or yellow peppers, deseeded and cut into strips
- 2 cloves of garlic, finely chopped
- 1 tsp paprika
- 1 x 250g pouch of ready cooked Smoky Spanish-Style Grains & Rice
- 150g green beans, topped and tailed
- Handful of parsley, roughly chopped, plus extra to serve
- Juice of 1 lemon, plus 1 extra lemon, quartered, to serve
- Salt and black pepper

METHOD

1. Stir the saffron into the hot vegetable stock and set aside to infuse.

2. Heat the oil in a saucepan over a medium–high heat and fry the onion for 4 minutes until soft. Add the peppers and cook for a further 8 minutes, then add the garlic and paprika and cook for 1–2 minutes.

3. Add the grains along with the saffron-infused vegetable stock. Bring to a boil, then simmer for 5 minutes until the stock has been absorbed.

4. Boil some water with a good pinch of salt in a medium saucepan, then add the green beans and cook for 2–3 minutes until tender. Drain, then add to the paella with the parsley and lemon juice.

5. Season the paella with salt and black pepper and serve straight to the table with lemon wedges and more parsley.

One-Pot & One-Tray Meals

ROAST NEW POTATOES WITH BELUGA LENTILS, SUN-DRIED TOMATOES & A LEMON DRESSING

Roasting the new potatoes makes them like mini jacket potatoes: crispy and golden on the outside and soft and pillowy in the middle.

 SERVES 4   40 MINS

INGREDIENTS

- 2 tsp sweet smoked paprika
- 4 sprigs of thyme, leaves picked, plus extra to garnish
- 1 tbsp maple syrup
- 3 tbsp olive oil
- 750g new potatoes
- 3 cloves of garlic, left whole in their skins
- 200g long-stem broccoli
- 1 x 250g pouch of ready cooked Beluga® Lentils
- 2 tbsp Sun-Dried Tomatoes in Sunflower Oil, chopped, plus 2 tbsp of their oil
- Handful of parsley, leaves picked
- Juice of ½ lemon
- Salt and black pepper

METHOD

1. Preheat the oven to 220°C (200°C fan)/Gas mark 7.

2. Mix the paprika, thyme, maple syrup and 2 tablespoons of the olive oil together in a small bowl until smooth.

3. Put the potatoes and garlic in a baking tray with the paprika mixture and toss well so that everything is coated, then roast for 25 minutes.

4. Remove from the oven and add the broccoli with another tablespoon of olive oil, then return to the oven for a further 10 minutes until the potatoes are golden and soft in the middle and the broccoli is tender.

5. Remove the garlic cloves from the tray, squeeze the roasted garlic from their papery outsides and add back to the roasting tray along with the lentils, sun-dried tomatoes and the 2 tablespoons of their oil, half the parsley, and the lemon juice. Season with salt and black pepper.

6. Toss everything together, then transfer to a warm serving platter and serve sprinkled with the remaining parsley and extra thyme leaves.

BAKED AUBERGINE, PUY LENTILS, BREADCRUMBS & HERBS

The aubergines are baked and served just like jacket potatoes, which go perfectly with the crispy roast lentils. By roasting the whole garlic bulb, you get the most delicious soft and sweet garlic. If you want, roast two bulbs so that you've got one spare in the fridge to add to dressings or stir into mayonnaise.

 SERVES 4   50 MINS

INGREDIENTS

- 1 x 250g pouch of ready cooked Puy Lentils
- 250g cherry tomatoes on the vine
- 1 tbsp harissa
- Zest and juice of 1 lemon
- 3 tbsp olive oil
- Salt and black pepper
- 4 aubergines, left whole
- 1 whole bulb of garlic
- 75g breadcrumbs
- Small handful of parsley, leaves picked
- Extra virgin olive oil, to drizzle

METHOD

1. Preheat the oven to 200°C (180°C fan)/Gas mark 6.

2. Squeeze the pouch slightly to loosen the lentils, then add them to a mixing bowl with the tomatoes, harissa, lemon zest and 2 tablespoons of the oil. Season with salt and black pepper. Toss everything together so that the lentils are evenly coated and set aside.

3. Put the aubergines and garlic in a large roasting tray and prick the aubergines a few times with the tip of a knife, then pour over the remaining tablespoon of oil and rub it all over the garlic and aubergines so they are evenly coated. Roast for 20 minutes.

4. Remove from the oven and add the breadcrumbs, lentils and tomatoes to the roasting tray in a single layer. Return to the oven for a further 20–25 minutes until the aubergines, garlic and tomatoes are really soft and the lentils are crispy.

5. Cut the aubergines in half lengthways, a bit like you'd do with a baked potato, and serve on a large platter with the tomatoes and crispy lentils. Squeeze the soft roasted garlic cloves from their papery sleeves onto the platter and garnish with the parsley, a good drizzle of extra virgin olive oil and a squeeze of lemon juice.

LENTIL & COURGETTE CAPONATA

This makes a hearty, comforting and zingy midweek meal. Caponata is the best dish for balancing sweet, sour and salty. If you want a more substantial meal, add the sauce into pasta with half a cup of pasta water to loosen it up.

 SERVES 4   50 MINS

INGREDIENTS

- 4 large tbsp olive oil, plus a little extra
- 3 large courgettes, cut into 1.5cm cubes
- 2 banana shallots, finely chopped
- 3 celery sticks, finely chopped
- 1 clove of garlic, finely chopped
- 150g dried Puy lentils
- 2 tbsp red wine vinegar
- 1 x 400g can plum tomatoes
- 200ml vegetable stock or water
- 12 Kalamata olives, pitted
- 2 tbsp capers
- Large handful of parsley, roughly chopped
- Small handful of basil, leaves pickled
- Salt and black pepper

To serve
- Extra virgin olive oil, for drizzling
- Crusty bread

METHOD

1. Heat the oil in a saucepan over a medium–high heat. Add the courgettes and cook for about 8 minutes until golden and soft, then remove from the pan.

2. Add the shallots, celery and garlic to the pan with a little more oil and cook for 5–6 minutes until translucent and soft.

3. Stir in the lentils and the vinegar, then the tomatoes, stock, courgettes, olives and capers and bring to the boil.

4. Once boiling, reduce the heat and simmer for 30 minutes until the lentils are soft and the sauce has reduced.

5. Stir in the parsley and half the basil and season with salt and black pepper. Serve with a little drizzle of extra virgin olive oil, the remaining basil leaves and some bread.

SPANISH ROAST ARTICHOKES & FENNEL

Roasting the vegetables with thin lemon slices makes all the difference –
the slices steam and caramelise around the fennel and artichokes, leaving
them with a perfect lemony flavour. You can discard the lemon slices
once they have been roasted or leave them in if you like their bitter taste.

 SERVES 4   35 MINS

INGREDIENTS

- 200g jar of artichokes in oil,
  drained and halved
- 2 fennel bulbs, each cut into
  8 wedges, fronds reserved
- 2 tbsp capers, drained
- 1 x 250g pouch of ready
  cooked Smoky Spanish-Style
  Grains & Rice
- 1 lemon, thinly sliced
- 2 cloves of garlic, crushed
- 2 tbsp olive oil
- Salt and black pepper

To serve
- Small bunch of parsley,
  leaves picked
- Small red chilli, deseeded
  and finely chopped
- 100g rocket
- 25g skin-on almonds,
  roughly chopped
- Extra virgin olive oil,
  to drizzle

METHOD

1. Preheat the oven to 220°C (200°C fan)/Gas mark 7.

2. In a large roasting tray, mix the artichokes, fennel,
capers, grains, lemon slices and garlic together with the oil.
Season with salt and black pepper. Roast for 30 minutes
until the artichokes and fennel are golden and the grains
slightly crispy.

3. Serve on a large platter with the parsley, chilli, rocket,
fennel fronds and chopped almonds. Finish with a drizzle
of oil.

GLORIOUS GRAINS MUSHROOM CONGEE

Congee is a savoury rice porridge often eaten for breakfast in parts of Asia. Traditionally, it's made with just rice but the grains and quinoa give it an interesting new texture. This is a fantastic, easy-to-cook lunch or dinner in the colder months and you can be really creative with the toppings too – crispy onions, garlic, ginger and chilli oil are a match made in heaven.

 SERVES 4   45 MINS

INGREDIENTS

- 4 dried shiitake mushrooms
- 50ml boiling water
- 100g long grain rice
- 1 tbsp olive oil
- 1 clove of garlic, finely chopped or grated
- Thumb-sized piece of ginger, peeled and grated
- 4 spring onions, thinly sliced
- 1 lemongrass stalk
- 1 x 250g pouch of ready cooked Glorious Grains with Red Rice & Quinoa
- 400ml good-quality vegetable stock
- Sea salt flakes and black pepper

Optional toppings
- Kimchi
- Coriander leaves
- Sesame seeds
- Spring onions, shredded
- Crispy onions
- Red chilli, finely chopped
- Chilli oil
- Steamed greens
- Pickled ginger

METHOD

1. Start by soaking the dried mushrooms in the boiling water for 10 minutes. Rinse the rice in a sieve until the water runs totally clear.

2. In a medium saucepan, heat the oil and fry the garlic, ginger and spring onions over medium heat for 2 minutes, or until soft.

3. Slice the lemongrass in half lengthways, then bash the ends with a rolling pin or push down and bruise with the back of a knife.

4. Once the mushrooms have steeped in the water, remove them (reserving the water) and finely chop.

5. Add the lemongrass, grains, rice, chopped mushrooms, sieved mushroom stock and vegetable stock to the saucepan with the ginger and garlic, then bring to a boil. Now lower the heat and gently simmer for 30 minutes, stirring often until the rice is creamy and soft. You want to almost overcook all the grains and rice to create a creamy, porridge texture, so don't be afraid to keep cooking until you're happy with the consistency.

6. Season the congee with salt and pepper then spoon into bowls and serve with a selection of toppings of your choice.

SEED & WHOLEGRAIN CRACKERS

These are a very addictive snack to have to hand when you just crave cheese or easy bits and pieces for lunch or dinner. The quantities here make a big batch as they will keep in an airtight container for up to two weeks. They are delicious dipped into hummus for a light snack. This recipe works really well with quinoa and any other spices or seeds that you like, so mix it up with what you've got in your cupboards.

 MAKES 2 SHEETS, BROKEN INTO PIECES   **1 HR**

INGREDIENTS

- 1 x 250g pouch of ready cooked Glorious Grains with Red Rice & Quinoa
- 25g pumpkin seeds
- 25g sesame seeds
- 25g sunflower seeds
- 25g poppy seeds
- 100g rolled oats
- 100g plain flour
- 30g chia seeds
- 2 tsp fennel seeds
- 1 tsp cumin seeds
- 1 tsp mustard seeds
- 1 tsp sea salt flakes
- 4 tbsp olive oil
- 300ml warm water

To serve
- Selection of vegan cheeses
- Green apple, thinly sliced
- Green or red grapes
- Cornichons or large pickles

METHOD

1. Preheat the oven to 200°C (180°C fan)/Gas mark 6.

2. Mix all the ingredients together in a large mixing bowl, stirring in the warm water last, until combined into a thick paste. Cover and set aside for 15 minutes, stirring occasionally, until you have a thick seedy mixture.

3. Lay out a large piece of parchment paper and dollop half the mixture into the middle. Lay another sheet of parchment paper on top and roll out the mixture into a 2mm thin even layer – the thinner the better. Repeat with the other half.

4. Transfer the rolled out dough to 2 baking sheets and remove the top layer of parchment from each. Bake for 20 minutes until golden on top, then carefully flip over and bake for a further 15–20 minutes until golden.

5. Allow to cool completely, then snap into pieces and serve with your favourite vegan cheeses, apple slices, grapes and cornichons.

TURMERIC ROAST CAULIFLOWER

A proper showstopper centrepiece dish for any occasion. Roasting the cauliflower in big chunks makes the outside charred, crisp and golden and the centre soft and tender. We love roasting the grains like this too, so that they are half crispy and half soft.

 SERVES 4 40 MINS

INGREDIENTS

- 1 medium whole cauliflower (weighing about 1kg)
- 1 tsp ground turmeric
- 1 tsp cumin seeds
- 1 tsp ground coriander
- 2 cloves of garlic, finely chopped
- 2 tbsp tomato purée
- Zest and juice of 1 lemon
- 4 tbsp olive oil
- Sea salt flakes and black pepper
- 1 x 250g pouch of ready cooked Glorious Grains with Red Rice & Quinoa
- Small bunch of parsley, leaves picked, plus extra to garnish
- Small bunch of mint, leaves picked, plus extra to garnish
- Handful of pomegranate seeds, plus extra to garnish
- Extra virgin olive oil, to drizzle
- 1 tbsp sumac

METHOD

1. Preheat the oven to 220°C (200°C fan)/Gas mark 7.

2. Trim the larger leaves off the cauliflower, leaving some of the smaller leaves on as they get really nice and crispy and taste delicious. Cut the cauliflower into 6 wedges and put in a large roasting tray.

3. Mix the spices, garlic, tomato purée, lemon zest and 2 tablespoons of the oil together in a bowl to make a loose paste, then rub it all over the cauliflower with your hands, so that it gets into all the cracks. Spread the cauliflower out so that each wedge has room around it, then season generously with salt and black pepper and roast for 20 minutes.

4. Remove the tray from the oven and add the grains, spreading them out around the cauliflower. Drizzle with the remaining oil, giving the grains a stir so they are coated, then return to the oven for another 15 minutes. The cauliflower should be a deep golden colour, slightly charred and tender in the middle.

5. Remove the cauliflower from the roasting tray and toss the parsley, mint, pomegranate seeds and lemon juice through the crispy grains. Drizzle with a little extra virgin olive oil.

6. Serve the cauliflower on top of the herby grains with an extra scattering of herbs, pomegranate seeds and sumac.

BAKED PUY LENTILS & RICE WITH CRISPY ONIONS, SUMAC & CUCUMBER

There's something amazing about crispy onions, rice and lentils that makes this dish so good. It is so easy to put together and is cooked in the oven with no lid for maximum crispy topping.

 SERVES 4    1 HR 10 MINS

INGREDIENTS

- 150g brown basmati rice or short grain brown rice
- 2 tbsp olive oil, plus extra for drizzling
- 2 large red onions, finely chopped
- 2 red peppers, deseeded and finely chopped
- 4 cloves of garlic, finely diced
- 1 tsp cumin seeds
- 2 tsp ground turmeric
- 1 tsp ground coriander
- 150g dried Puy lentils
- 750ml hot vegetable stock
- Sea salt flakes and black pepper
- Zest and juice of 1 lemon

To serve
- Handful of coriander, parsley and mint, leaves picked
- ½ cucumber, diced
- Pinch of chilli flakes or ½ deseeded red chilli, finely chopped
- 1 tsp sumac
- Handful of crispy onions, or make your own (page 40)

METHOD

1. Preheat the oven to 200°C (180°C fan)/Gas mark 6.

2. Wash the rice in a sieve until the water runs clear, then set aside.

3. Heat the oil in a medium (about 30cm) non-stick ovenproof frying pan and fry the onions and red peppers for 10–15 minutes until the onions are really soft and slightly caramelised.

4. Add the garlic and spices and cook for a further 3 minutes to release the flavours, then tip in the lentils and rice and stir, making sure everything is evenly coated. Cover with the stock and season well with salt and black pepper.

5. Bring to the boil, then place in the oven, without a lid, for 40–50 minutes until the rice is cooked and the top is getting crispy.

6. Remove from the oven, drizzle with a little oil and place on a medium heat on the hob for a few minutes so the bottom gets crispy too, being mindful not to burn it.

7. Remove from the heat and squeeze over half the lemon juice and check the seasoning.

8. To serve, scatter the herbs, cucumber, chilli flakes, sumac, lemon zest and crispy onions on top of the baked lentils and rice and add the remaining lemon juice.

MEXICAN-STYLE STUFFED TOMATOES

You need large tomatoes for this, so use the beef tomatoes that are about 6cm wide. You might only find them in summer when they are in season, so if you can't find them, swap the tomatoes for peppers.

 SERVES 6   45 MINS

INGREDIENTS

- 6 large beef tomatoes
- 3 tbsp olive oil, plus extra for drizzling
- 1 medium onion, finely chopped
- 1 tsp tomato purée
- 1 x 250g pouch of ready cooked Spicy Mexican-Style Grains
- Small handful of coriander, finely chopped
- Small handful of parsley, finely chopped
- Zest and juice of 1 lemon
- Salt and black pepper

To serve
- Green salad

METHOD

1. Preheat the oven to 200°C (180°C fan)/Gas mark 6.

2. Cut the tops off the tomatoes and carefully scoop out the soft pulp into a bowl, chopping up any larger pieces (reserve the tops).

3. Heat the oil in an ovenproof frying pan or shallow casserole over a medium heat and fry the onion for 5–7 minutes until soft. Stir in the tomato pulp, tomato purée and grains.

4. Remove the casserole from the heat and stir in the coriander, parsley and lemon juice and zest and season with salt and black pepper.

5. Fill each tomato shell with the grains mixture until the frying pan is empty, then place the tomatoes, with their tops back on, in the frying pan. Drizzle with oil and roast in the oven for 30 minutes until the tomatoes are soft and blistered on top.

6. Serve with a green salad.

PERSIAN ROAST SQUASH

This is a lovely dish to serve guests at any time of the year. It's worth roasting the squash in two halves as you can scoop out the flesh, which becomes buttery and sweet, at the table.

 SERVES 4   1 HR

INGREDIENTS

- 1kg squash
- 1 whole bulb of garlic
- 4 tbsp olive oil, plus a little extra
- 1 tsp ground cumin
- 1 tsp ground coriander
- 1 x 250g pouch of ready cooked Aromatic Persian-Style Quinoa & Lentils
- Handful of parsley, leaves picked
- Handful of coriander, leaves picked
- Handful of mint, leaves picked

For the dressing
- 6 tbsp extra virgin olive oil
- Zest and juice of ½ lemon
- 1 tbsp zaatar, plus extra to serve
- Salt and black pepper

To serve
- 100g pistachios, roughly chopped
- 1 tbsp sumac

METHOD

1. Preheat the oven to 200°C (180°C fan)/Gas mark 6.

2. Halve the squash lengthways and scoop out the seeds. Don't worry about peeling it as the skin holds it together as it roasts.

3. Put the squash halves in a large roasting tray with the garlic bulb, oil, cumin and coriander. Using your hands, rub the spices and oil all over the squash and garlic so they are totally coated, then roast for 20–25 minutes until completely soft.

4. Remove the tray from the oven and tip the grains around the squash, then drizzle with a little more oil and return to the oven for another 20–25 minutes.

5. Carefully remove the squash and garlic from the roasting tray and squeeze the soft roasted garlic cloves out of their skins and mix them with all the dressing ingredients.

6. Drizzle the dressing over the warm grains and add the herbs. Season with salt and black pepper and spoon onto a large serving platter.

7. Place the whole pieces of squash on top of the grains and scatter with the pistachios, a little more zaatar and the sumac. Slice the squash into chunks or scoop out the flesh to serve.

TOMATO & CAPER TART WITH CHESTNUT TAPENADE

This is a go-to summer lunch that never gets old. If you don't use all the tapenade, it can be kept in an airtight jar in the fridge for two weeks to enjoy on toast or as a dip. This tart looks amazing with heirloom tomatoes in different shapes and sizes, but regular red tomatoes are equally delicious.

 SERVES 4 35 MINS

INGREDIENTS

- 1 x 320g vegan ready-rolled puff pastry sheet
- 400g tomatoes (use different colours, shapes or sizes), sliced
- 2 sprigs of fresh oregano
- 1 tbsp capers
- 2 tbsp any vegan milk
- Extra virgin olive oil, to drizzle
- Salt and black pepper

For the chestnut tapenade
- 1 clove of garlic
- 4 tbsp capers
- 50g black olives, pitted
- Small bunch of parsley
- Small handful of fresh oregano or thyme
- 1 x 200g pouch of Chestnut Purée
- 2–4 tbsp extra virgin olive oil

METHOD

1. Preheat the oven to 220°C (200°C fan)/Gas mark 7.

2. If you like a textured tapenade, just chop everything on a chopping board and mix together with the chestnut purée, adding enough oil to form a paste. (This also works really well in a pestle and mortar.) If you like a smoother paste, put all the ingredients in a blender and blitz until you have the desired consistency, adding olive oil as you go.

3. Spread the puff pastry out onto a cold baking tray lined with parchment paper and lightly score a border around the edges of the pastry using the back of a knife. Be light here as you don't want to score all the way through the pastry.

4. Evenly spread the tapenade inside the border, then transfer any remaining tapenade into an airtight jar to enjoy over the next 2 weeks.

5. Lay the tomatoes over the tapenade, with the larger slices first and then some smaller ones on top. Scatter over the sprigs of oregano and the capers.

6. Using a pastry brush, brush the borders of the pastry with the milk. Drizzle the tart with extra virgin olive oil, and season with salt and black pepper.

7. Bake for 25 minutes, or until puffed up and golden.

Big
Feasts

FALAFELS WITH HUMMUS & FLATBREADS

Everyone loves a falafel feast! The quinoa in these makes for the best crispy outer layer of the falafels with the softest inside. You can add loads more sides if you want to, like pickled red cabbage, tomatoes and lettuce.

 SERVES 4   1 HR 30 MINS

INGREDIENTS

For the falafels
- 1 x 250g pouch of ready cooked Red & White Quinoa
- 1 x 400g can chickpeas, drained and rinsed
- 2 cloves of garlic, peeled
- 1 small onion, diced
- Small handful of parsley
- Small handful of coriander
- 1 tsp ground cumin
- 1 tsp ground coriander
- 2 tbsp sesame seeds
- 4 tbsp plain flour, plus extra for dusting
- 1 tsp baking powder
- Salt and black pepper
- Vegetable oil, for frying

For the flatbreads
- 300ml lukewarm water
- 7g sachet of dried yeast
- 1 tbsp sugar
- 500g strong white bread flour
- 2 tsp salt
- 3 tbsp olive oil

For the hummus
- 1 x 400g can chickpeas, drained and rinsed
- Juice of 1 lemon
- 1 clove of garlic, finely chopped
- 2 tbsp tahini
- 2–4 tbsp best extra virgin olive oil

To serve – pick and choose!
- ½ cucumber, diced
- Handful of herbs such as mint, dill, parsley and coriander
- 1 tsp sumac
- 1 tsp zaatar
- Pickled chillies (optional)

METHOD

1. Add all the falafel ingredients, minus the vegetable oil, to a food processor and blitz until combined but not totally smooth. The mixture should form a rough dough that can be rolled into a small ball and doesn't stick to your hands. Put the mixture in a bowl, cover and refrigerate for at least 1 hour or overnight.

2. In the meantime, make the flatbread dough. Mix the warm water, yeast and sugar together and leave for a few minutes to help the yeast activate and foam up a little.

3. Add the flour to a large mixing bowl with the salt, then make a well in the centre. Pour the yeast mixture and the oil into the middle of the flour, then slowly bring the flour from the edge into the middle until you end up with a shaggy dough.

Continued...

4. Tip the dough onto a clean work surface and knead for about 10 minutes until smooth, soft and springy. (Or use a stand mixer and mix with the dough hook for 6–7 minutes.) Put the dough in a clean, lightly oiled bowl, cover and leave in a warm place for 1 hour or until doubled in size.

5. For the hummus, drain the chickpeas but reserve the liquid. Put the chickpeas, lemon juice, garlic, tahini and 3 tablespoons of the chickpea water into a food processor. Blend for a few seconds before adding the oil, 1 tablespoon at a time, until you have a smooth and creamy texture. Season with salt and black pepper, adding more lemon juice if you think it needs it. Spoon into a small serving bowl and set aside.

6. Once the dough has risen and the falafel mixture has cooled, shape the falafel mixture into golf ball-sized patties and set aside.

7. Divide the flatbread dough into 8 even-sized balls and place onto a lightly floured tray to prove for another 10 minutes, then roll out each ball to a 15cm circle. Heat a large frying pan to a medium–high heat, then dry-fry each flatbread for 2 minutes on each side until deep golden and risen slightly. Set aside, wrapped in a tea towel to keep warm.

8. Heat the vegetable oil in a medium, high-sided, heavy-based saucepan until it reaches about 180°C. If you don't have a food thermometer, just drop a little of the mixture into the oil and if it sizzles, you're ready to go. Be careful not to overheat the oil: you want the falafels to be golden outside with a soft centre; if the oil is too hot, you'll burn the outside and the centre will remain cold.

9. Carefully add the falafels 3 or 4 at a time so as to not overcrowd the pan, and fry for about 3 minutes until golden brown and crispy. Drain on kitchen paper and repeat with the remaining falafels.

10. Serve the falafels on a large serving platter with a pile of the flatbreads, the hummus and your choice of sides.

ITALIAN GRAIN ARANCINI BALLS

This is the easiest arancini recipe, thanks to the pre-cooked grains pouch! The risotto filling is ready in minutes with no compromise on flavour. The better the vegan cheese, the better the arancini, so go for the best one.

 SERVES 4   1 HR 20 MINS

INGREDIENTS

- 2 tbsp olive oil
- 1 onion, finely chopped
- 1 clove of garlic, finely chopped
- 1 x 250g pouch of ready cooked Herby Italian-Style Grains
- 50ml vegan white wine
- Salt and black pepper
- 2 handfuls of vegan cheddar or mozzarella

- Zest and juice of 1 lemon
- 1 tbsp plain flour
- 500ml vegetable oil, for frying

For the pesto
- 50g pine nuts
- Large bunch of basil
- 2 tbsp nutritional yeast
- 125ml extra virgin olive oil

- 1 small clove of garlic
- Zest and juice of ½ lemon

For the breadcrumbs
- 4 tbsp plain flour
- 50ml vegan milk
- 100g fine breadcrumbs

Continued...

METHOD

1. Heat the olive oil in a medium frying pan over a medium heat and gently fry the onion for about 5 minutes until soft. Add the garlic and fry for a few more minutes, then stir in the grains, making sure you've squeezed the pouch slightly to loosen the grains beforehand. Cook for a few minutes, then add the wine. Once the wine is absorbed, season well, then add the cheese, lemon zest and juice, and the flour. Remove from the heat, spread the mixture out on a tray and refrigerate for 1 hour until you're ready to cook.

2. To make the pesto, dry-fry the pine nuts for 2–3 minutes, then remove from the heat and let cool. Add the pine nuts with the remaining ingredients to a food processor and blitz a few times until combined. Transfer to a bowl, ready for serving.

3. Get your bread-crumbing station set up by having 3 bowls to hand: tip the flour into one bowl, the milk into another and the breadcrumbs into a third.

4. Using your hands, shape the mixture into 8 even-sized balls (roughly 40g each), compressing the grains tightly so they stick together. Roll each ball in the flour, then dip in the milk and finally roll in the breadcrumbs. Set the balls aside.

5. Heat the vegetable oil in a medium, high-sided, heavy-based saucepan over a medium–high heat. The oil should reach about 180°C, but if you don't have a food thermometer, just test the oil by dropping in a few breadcrumbs or a little of the mixture – if it sizzles, then you're good to go.

6. Line a tray with kitchen paper, then carefully drop the balls, 3 or 4 at a time, into the oil so as not to overcrowd the pan. Fry for 3–4 minutes, turning occasionally so they are evenly golden.

7. Remove the arancini from the oil using a slotted spoon and season with salt while they are still hot. Repeat to cook the remaining arancini and serve with the pesto for dipping.

SPICY MEXICAN GRAIN TACOS WITH ROAST CELERIAC, PICKLED RADISHES & AVOCADO

The spicy grains and pulses hold all the flavour you need in these tacos – spicy and limey with crunchy bits of corn. For a truly authentic Mexican flavour, get the proper corn tacos as they make all the difference.

 SERVES 4   1 HR

INGREDIENTS

- 1 small celeriac, peeled and cut into 2cm chunks
- 1 tbsp chipotle paste
- 2 tbsp olive oil
- Salt and black pepper
- 1 x 250g pouch of ready cooked Spicy Mexican-Style Grains

For the pickled radishes
- 100g radishes, very thinly sliced
- 2 tbsp red wine vinegar or juice of ½ lemon

For the chipotle mayonnaise
- 1 tbsp chipotle paste
- 4 tbsp vegan mayonnaise
- Juice of ½ lime

To serve
- 2 avocados
- 2 limes, quartered
- 8 small corn tacos
- 1 small white onion, very finely diced
- Small handful of coriander, leaves picked

METHOD

1. Preheat the oven to 220°C (200°C fan)/Gas mark 7.

2. Add the celeriac, chipotle paste and oil to a roasting tray and season with salt and black pepper. Toss together until the celeriac is coated in the flavours, then roast for 20 minutes. Remove from the oven and add the grains. Give everything a stir, then return to the oven for a further 15 minutes until the celeriac is soft and caramelised.

3. While the celeriac is roasting, put the radishes and vinegar in a small bowl and mix together so that the radishes turn pink all over, then set aside to pickle.

4. To make the chipotle mayonnaise, stir all the ingredients together in a small bowl and set aside.

5. Stone, peel and slice the avocados, then squeeze over the juice of half a lime to stop the flesh from browning.

6. Wrap the tacos in foil and warm in a low oven or between 2 plates in the microwave, then wrap in a clean tea towel to keep warm.

7. Spoon the celeriac and grains into a large serving bowl and all the other bits into separate bowls and allow everyone to build their own tacos.

POTATO, LENTIL & SPINACH CURRY

The crispy, roast new potatoes take this curry to the next level. Squashing them halfway through roasting creates even more surface for crispiness, making them soft and pillowy in the middle and golden on the outside.

 SERVES 4   1 HR

INGREDIENTS

For the potatoes
- 500g new potatoes, large ones halved
- 2 tbsp olive oil
- 1 tsp mustard seeds
- 1 tsp ground coriander
- 1 tsp ground cumin
- Salt and black pepper

For the curry
- 2 tbsp olive oil
- 3 onions, halved and finely sliced
- 3 cloves of garlic, finely chopped
- Thumb-sized piece of ginger, peeled and grated or finely chopped
- 1 tsp ground turmeric
- 2 tsp ground cumin
- 1 tsp mustard seeds
- 1 x 250g pouch of ready cooked Puy Lentils
- 1 x 400ml can full-fat coconut milk
- 300g spinach
- Zest and juice of 1 lemon

To serve
- 4 naan breads
- 50g toasted cashew nuts, roughly chopped

METHOD

1. Preheat the oven to 220°C (200°C fan)/Gas mark 7.

2. Add the potatoes to a roasting tray and toss them in the oil and spices. Season generously with salt and black pepper and roast for 20 minutes.

3. Remove from the oven and, using the back of a fork, lightly squash the potatoes so they burst and flatten a little. Return to the oven for a further 10–15 minutes until crispy and golden.

4. While the potatoes are roasting, make the curry. Heat the oil in a large non-stick frying pan over a medium heat and gently fry the onions for 8–10 minutes until they are really soft. Reduce the heat a little and stir in the garlic and ginger and cook for a further 8 minutes, being careful not to burn the garlic.

5. Add the spices to the onion mixture and fry for a few minutes until fragrant. Stir in the lentils and coconut milk, season and simmer for 10–15 minutes until reduced to a thick sauce. Once you're happy with the consistency, add the spinach and lemon juice and cook until the spinach is wilted. Remove from the heat and stir in the crispy potatoes, holding back a few for the top.

6. Serve with naan bread, and sprinkled with the lemon zest and cashew nuts.

CHESTNUT, SAGE & POTATO PIZZETTE

This is sort of a hybrid of garlic bread, crisps and pizza in one. You can play around with the toppings too. Thinly sliced courgettes or mushrooms would be delicious.

 SERVES 4-6   3 HRS

INGREDIENTS

For the dough
- 300ml lukewarm water
- 7g sachet of dried yeast
- 1 tbsp caster sugar
- 500g strong white bread flour or 00 flour, plus extra for dusting
- 1 tsp fine sea salt
- 2 tbsp of good-quality extra virgin olive oil, plus extra for greasing

For the topping
- 2 small Maris Piper potatoes
- 1 small fennel bulb
- 3 tbsp extra virgin olive oil
- 1 clove of garlic, very finely chopped
- Small handful of parsley leaves, finely chopped
- 1 x 180g pouch of ready cooked Whole Chestnuts, roughly chopped
- Small handful of sage leaves
- Salt and black pepper

METHOD

1. For the dough, mix the warm water with the yeast and sugar and leave for a few minutes to foam a little. Add the flour to a large bowl with the salt, then make a well in the centre. Pour the yeast mixture and oil into the well, then slowly bring the flour from the edges into the middle until you end up with a shaggy dough.

2. Tip the dough onto a clean work surface and knead for 10 minutes until smooth, soft and springy. (Or use a stand mixer and mix with the dough hook for 6–7 minutes.) Put the dough in a clean, lightly oiled bowl, cover and leave in a warm place for 1 hour or until doubled in size.

3. Meanwhile, make the topping. Very thinly slice the potatoes and fennel – the thinner the better. This is best done using a mandolin, but a sharp knife will do. In a small bowl, mix the oil, garlic and parsley together, then set aside.

4. Preheat the grill to medium.

5. Tip the dough out onto a well-floured surface and divide it into 6 equal pieces, then roll out into 10cm discs.

6. Place a disc of dough in a dry ovenproof frying pan and carefully spread out a little using your fingers. Spoon on 1–2 tablespoons of the garlic oil, spreading it out with the back of a spoon to cover the base. Place the pan over a high heat to crisp up the bottom for 2–3 minutes, then add one-sixth of the potatoes and fennel in a single layer, followed by one-sixth of the chestnuts and sage and a little more garlic oil.

7. Season with salt and black pepper, then place the pan under the grill for 5–10 minutes until the potatoes and fennel are golden, soft, and crisp at the edges and the dough has risen. Remove from the grill, keep warm in a low oven and repeat with the remaining dough.

WINTER SQUASH, SHALLOT & CHESTNUT TART

This could be a Christmas day showstopper or just a casual lunch – it's easy to prepare and looks impressive on the table. You could even cut the pastry into four for individual tarts if you wanted. The salsa verde recipe makes a lot, but you'll be surprised how much of it you'll want; if any is left over, it keeps in the fridge for a few days and is delicious with most things.

 SERVES 4   1 HR 10 MINS

INGREDIENTS

- 3 banana shallots, trimmed and halved lengthways
- 600g onion squash or butternut squash, deseeded and cut into thin 2cm wedges (peeled if you prefer)
- 5 cloves of garlic, left whole
- 2 tbsp chopped thyme, plus extra to sprinkle
- 2 tbsp olive oil
- Salt and black pepper
- 1 x 320g vegan ready-rolled puff pastry sheet
- 1 x 180g pouch of ready cooked Whole Chestnuts, roughly chopped
- Vegan milk, for brushing

For the salsa verde
- 1 clove of garlic
- 2 large handfuls of parsley
- Small handful of basil
- Small handful of mint
- 2 tbsp capers
- 1 tbsp mustard
- 120ml best extra virgin olive oil
- Juice of 1 lemon

METHOD

1. Preheat the oven to 220°C (200°C fan)/Gas mark 7.

2. Arrange the shallots, squash, thyme and garlic in a large baking tray. Toss everything in the oil, season and roast for 25–30 minutes until almost tender. Reduce the heat to 200°C (180°C fan)/Gas mark 6.

3. Lay out the pastry on another baking tray and lightly score a 1cm border around the edges, making sure you don't cut all the way through.

4. Spread the roasted vegetables over the pastry within the border, making sure they don't overlap too much, then crumble over the chestnuts and a little more thyme. Brush the edges with the milk, then return to the oven for 30 minutes until the pastry is risen and golden and the squash and onions are caramelised and soft.

5. To make the salsa verde, add all the ingredients, except the oil and lemon juice, to a food processor and blitz until the garlic, herbs and capers are evenly chopped. Transfer to a bowl and stir in the oil and lemon juice until you're happy with the consistency. Season to taste, adding more lemon or oil if you need to.

6. Serve the tart in the middle of the table with a dollop of salsa verde and a green salad, if you like.

PUY LENTIL, MUSHROOM & CHESTNUT WELLINGTON WITH ALL THE TRIMMINGS

This is great served as a Sunday roast but also works really well as smaller versions too – just slice up into portions before baking for miniature rolls.

 SERVES 6    2 HRS 15 MINS

INGREDIENTS

- 3 tbsp olive oil, plus extra for frying
- 1 medium onion, finely chopped
- 250g chestnut mushrooms, roughly chopped
- 2 medium cloves of garlic, crushed
- 3 sage leaves, roughly chopped
- 1 tsp thyme leaves
- 2 x 250g pouches of ready cooked Puy Lentils
- 1 x 180g pouch of ready roasted Whole Chestnuts
- 1 tsp sweet smoked paprika
- 150g firm tofu, drained and grated
- 100g plain flour
- Salt and black pepper
- 500g vegan ready-rolled puff pastry sheets
- Vegan milk, for brushing

For the roast potatoes
- 1kg medium potatoes, such as Maris Piper
- 2 tbsp salt
- 5 tbsp olive oil
- 1 whole bulb of garlic
- 4 sprigs of rosemary

To serve
- Seasonal greens

METHOD

1. Preheat the oven to 200°C (180°C fan)/Gas mark 6.

2. Start by making the wellington filling. Heat the oil in a medium frying pan over a medium heat and fry the onion and mushrooms for 10–15 minutes until all the moisture has evaporated and the vegetables start to turn golden. Add the garlic, sage and thyme and fry for 2 more minutes, then remove from the heat and allow to cool for a few minutes.

3. Add the lentils and 100g of the chestnuts to a food processor and blitz until roughly chopped. Then add the onion and mushroom mixture, the paprika, tofu and flour and pulse a few more times until combined. Season with salt and black pepper, then chill in the fridge for 30 minutes.

Continued...

4. Line a baking tray with greaseproof paper and lay the pastry out on it. Crumble over the remaining chestnuts and press them into the pastry. Flip the pastry over so that the chestnuts are facing down, then lay a thick layer of the filling down one long side, leaving a 2cm border on the filling side so you can seal it.

5. Lift the unfilled side of the pastry up over the filling to meet the other side. Crimp the edge using the back of a fork, like a big sausage roll. With the back of a knife, score lines on top of the wellington and brush all over with milk. Season with salt and black pepper, then pop in the fridge while you get on the roast potatoes.

6. Peel the potatoes, keeping most of them whole but halving any that are too big. Place them in a large saucepan filled with cold water and add the salt. Bring to the boil for 15 minutes until they are very nearly cooked through. Drain in a colander, then leave to steam for 5 minutes. Now give the potatoes a shake in the colander until all the edges fluff up and have texture.

7. Pour the oil into a large roasting tray and heat it up for 5 minutes in the oven. Very carefully add the potatoes to the hot tray with the whole garlic bulb and rosemary and season with salt and black pepper, tossing the potatoes a little in the pan so they are coated in the oil. Spread them out evenly so there is space around each potato and roast for 45 minutes until golden and crispy. Remove from the oven and lightly squash the potatoes with a potato masher or the back of a fork to add extra crispiness. Return to the oven for a further 15 minutes.

8. At this point, remove the wellington from the fridge and place it on the top shelf of the oven. Cook for 30–35 minutes until the pastry is golden and risen.

9. Serve the wellington with the roast potatoes and seasonal greens.

CRISPY WHOLEGRAIN FOCACCIA

This is a go-to for a dinner party as it involves limited effort and maximum flavour! A good tip here is to make sure the yeast isn't old – don't use an already-opened sachet because you won't get as good a rise. This recipe works equally well with plain flour, spelt flour or even 00 flour, so use what you've got. You can top this focaccia with any grain, or anything you like, so get creative! This freezes really well once baked, so wrap any leftovers in clingfilm and freeze – simply warm in the oven when you are ready to eat the rest.

 SERVES 10-12    OVERNIGHT + 2 HRS

INGREDIENTS

For the dough
- 550ml lukewarm water
- ½ tsp active dry yeast
- 50ml best extra virgin olive oil, plus extra for greasing and finishing
- 2 tsp caster sugar or maple syrup
- 750g strong white bread flour
- ½ tbsp sea salt

For the topping
- 1 x 250g pouch of ready cooked Smoky Spanish-Style Grains & Rice
- 2 sprigs of rosemary, leaves picked
- Small handful of cherry tomatoes, halved
- Sea salt flakes

For the brine
- ½ tsp salt
- 25ml lukewarm water

METHOD

1. You will need to make the dough the night before you want to bake and serve the focaccia. Stir the water, yeast, oil and sugar together in a jug to dissolve, then leave for 10 minutes for the yeast to activate a little.

Continued...

129

2. In a large mixing bowl, mix the flour and salt together, then pour in the yeast mixture. Mix everything together so that there are no lumps of flour, then scrape the sides of the bowl clean with a spatula and cover with a tea towel or clingfilm, making sure the bowl is large enough for the dough to double in size. Leave at room temperature for 12–14 hours, or until at least doubled in volume.

3. The next morning, put 2–3 large tablespoons of oil into a 40 x 30cm high-sided roasting tray. Very very carefully, scrape the dough into the tray using a spatula, making sure you keep all the air bubbles that have developed overnight. Rub 2 tablespoons of olive oil over the dough and gently stretch it to the edges of the tray. Leave to rest in a warm place for 30 minutes, covered.

4. Squeeze the pouch slightly to loosen the grains, then sprinkle them evenly over the top of the dough, along with the rosemary and cherry tomatoes. It may seem like a lot of grains, but you'll get an amazing crispy top. Drizzle with a little more olive oil.

5. Grease your hands with oil, then press your fingers into the dough every 3cm or so all the way down the focaccia, pushing some of the grains into the dough.

6. Make the brine by stirring the salt into the warm water until dissolved, then lightly brush this all over the dough and its dimples – this creates the lovely salty crust on top. Rest for 45 minutes until risen again.

7. It should be really lovely and bubbly by now, but if it's a cold day and the dough hasn't risen as much as it should, just give it a little more time to prove. Meanwhile, preheat the oven to 220°C (200°C fan)/Gas mark 7.

8. Drizzle with a little more oil and season with a generous scattering of sea salt flakes, then bake for 30 minutes, or until all sides are golden brown and crispy.

9. Remove from the oven, then leave to cool in the tin for 10 minutes before removing with a palette knife. Slice and enjoy warm or leave to cool for later.

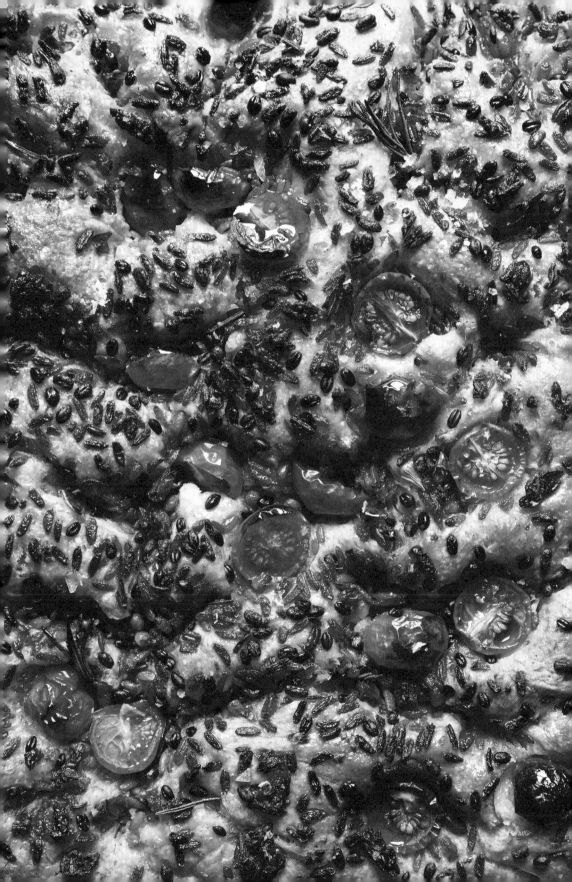

CAJUN-INSPIRED BEAN BURGERS

These burgers are far from boring. They are packed with flavour and can be prepared in minutes. If you like things spicy, add a chopped fresh red chilli to the burger mixture or a pickled jalapeño to serve.

 SERVES 4   1 HR

INGREDIENTS

For the burgers
- 3 tbsp olive oil
- 1 red onion, finely diced
- 2 cloves of garlic, finely chopped
- 1 tsp sweet smoked paprika
- 1 tsp ground cumin
- 2 x 250g pouches of ready cooked Spicy Cajun-Style Lentils & Kidney Beans
- 100g fresh breadcrumbs
- Salt and black pepper

For the corn salsa
- 2 corn on the cob
- Juice of 1 lime
- Small handful of coriander
- 1 tbsp extra virgin olive oil
- 1 tsp harissa

For the guacamole
- 1 avocado
- Juice of 1 lime
- Handful of coriander leaves, chopped
- 1 small red onion, finely chopped
- 2 tbsp extra virgin olive oil

To serve
- 4 burger buns
- Vegan mayonnaise
- 1–2 tomatoes, sliced
- 8 Little Gem lettuce leaves

METHOD

1. Start by making the burgers. Heat 2 tablespoons of the oil in a frying pan over a medium–high heat and fry the onion for 5 minutes until soft. Add the garlic and cook for 2 minutes, then add the spices, stirring them in for 1–2 minutes until fragrant. Remove from the heat. Add the lentils, breadcrumbs and onion mixture to a food processor with a generous pinch of salt and black pepper, then blitz a few times until combined but still with some texture.

2. Divide the mixture into 4 equal portions, shape into patties, then chill in the fridge for at least 30 minutes.

3. Meanwhile, make the salsa. Char the corn on a very hot griddle pan or under a hot grill for 6–8 minutes until tender, then slice off the kernels into a bowl. Add the lime juice, coriander, oil and harissa. Season with salt and black pepper and mix together.

4. Preheat the oven to 200°C (180°C fan)/Gas mark 6.

5. When you're ready to cook the burgers, heat the remaining oil in a large frying pan over a medium–high heat. Add the burgers and fry for 3–4 minutes on each side until golden, then transfer to a baking tray and place in the oven for 5 minutes to cook through.

6. Wipe down the frying pan using kitchen paper, then toast the burger buns, cut-side down, in the dry, hot pan until golden and toasted. Spread with vegan mayonnaise.

7. Mash all the guacamole ingredients together in a bowl and season with salt and pepper. Place in the middle of the table with the corn salsa, tomatoes, lettuce, buns and burgers for everyone to build their own.

ZINGY KOREAN-STYLE GRAIN GYOZAS

It's fun to sit at the kitchen table with family or friends to make these. There are so many ways to shape them, so if you want to be creative, have a look online for other ideas.

 MAKES 16 (SERVES 4)   **1 HR**

INGREDIENTS

- 2 tbsp sesame oil
- 6 spring onions, sliced
- 150g chestnut mushrooms, finely chopped
- 2 cloves of garlic, finely chopped
- Thumb-sized piece of ginger, peeled and chopped
- 1 x 250g pouch of ready cooked Zingy Korean-style Grains
- Small handful of coriander, finely chopped
- 16 gyoza wrappers
- 1 tbsp rice flour
- 50ml boiling water
- 2 tbsp olive oil

For the sweet chilli dip
- 2 tbsp mirin
- 2 tbsp rice vinegar
- 1 tbsp caster sugar
- 3 tbsp soy sauce
- ½ tbsp sesame oil
- 2 tbsp sweet chilli sauce

METHOD

1. Heat the sesame oil in a large frying pan over a medium heat and fry the spring onions for 1 minute, then add the mushrooms. Fry for 6–8 minutes until they have released all their liquid and become golden, adding a little more oil if needed. Add the garlic and ginger and fry for a further 2–3 minutes, then remove from the heat. Transfer the mushroom mixture to a bowl with the grains and stir in the coriander.

2. Place a gyoza wrapper in the palm of your hand. Add a big tablespoon of the mixture to the middle of the wrapper and, using your finger, brush the edges with a little water. Fold one side over the filling – you should have a semi-circle now. Start at one end of the semi-circle and pinch together the 2 edges, continuing along the seam until you reach the end – it should be slightly pleated. If this is too hard, you can just fold the 2 sides together and press shut!

3. Place the gyozas flat-side down on a tray, so that the seal is at the top and repeat with the remaining mixture and wrappers, then refrigerate for 30 minutes.

4. In a small bowl, mix together the rice flour with the boiling water and set aside.

5. Heat a heavy-based frying pan over a medium heat and add the gyozas in a neat single layer, then pour over 100ml water. Cover with a lid and steam for 7 minutes.

6. Remove the lid and add the rice flour and water mixture to the pan and increase the heat. Add the olive oil and fry for 2–3 minutes until the water evaporates and leaves you with a crispy skirt under the gyozas. Remove from the heat and repeat if doing in batches.

7. Mix all the dipping ingredients together in a small bowl, and serve with the gyozas.

LENTIL HUMMUS WITH MAPLE ROASTED CARROTS

Don't rush cooking the onion as it needs to be super soft and caramelised for maximum flavour before adding the other ingredients. This is a test of patience, but you won't regret it.

 SERVES 4   45 MINS

INGREDIENTS

For the roasted carrots
- 400g carrots, unpeeled but scrubbed, large ones halved lengthways
- 1 tbsp maple syrup
- 4 tbsp olive oil
- 1 tsp cumin seeds
- 1 tsp coriander seeds
- Salt and black pepper

For the hummus
- 1 x 400g can butter beans, drained and rinsed
- 4 tbsp extra virgin olive oil
- 1 large onion, very finely sliced
- 1 clove of garlic, roughly chopped
- 1 x 250g pouch of ready cooked Puy Lentils
- 2 tbsp tahini
- Juice of ½ lemon

To serve
- Extra virgin olive oil
- Quinoa dukkah (see page 44)

METHOD

1. Preheat the oven to 200°C (180°C fan)/Gas mark 6.

2. Add the carrots to a large roasting tray. In a small bowl, mix the maple syrup, oil, cumin and coriander seeds together and season with salt and black pepper. Pour over the carrots and toss so they are all coated, then roast for 25–30 minutes until tender and golden.

3. Drain the butter beans but reserve the liquid for later – this will get you the perfect smooth dip.

4. Heat 2 tablespoons of the oil in a frying pan over a medium heat and fry the onion for 10–15 minutes until really soft and caramelised, then add the garlic and cook for a further 2 minutes before adding the butter beans and lentils.

5. Remove the pan from the heat and transfer the lentil mixture to a food processor with the tahini and lemon juice. Then, with the motor running, slowly add 2 tablespoons of the butter bean liquid and the remaining 2 tablespoons of oil until you have the consistency you want – the hummus should be thick enough to hold its shape when stirred. Season generously with salt and black pepper and set aside.

6. Dollop the hummus onto a large platter, then spread it out using the back of a spoon. Pile the roasted carrots on top followed by a drizzle of oil and a scattering of dukkah.

Sweet
Eats

CHERRY POLENTA CAKE

This cake is so versatile that you can add any fruit you like – blueberries, raspberries or even peeled and chopped apples. Frozen cherries also work perfectly well here, so don't worry if they aren't in season.

 SERVES 8   50 MINS

INGREDIENTS

- 110ml neutral oil, such as sunflower or groundnut oil, plus extra for oiling
- 200g self-raising flour
- 150g simply ground Polenta
- 225g caster sugar
- 1 tsp bicarbonate of soda
- 1 tsp baking powder
- Small pinch of sea salt
- 200g cherries, pitted
- Zest and juice of 1 lemon
- 250ml almond milk
- 2 tbsp demerara sugar
- 50g almonds, roughly chopped

METHOD

1. Preheat the oven to 160°C (140°C fan)/Gas mark 3.

2. Oil the base and sides of a 23cm round loose-bottomed cake tin and line the base with non-stick parchment paper.

3. In a large bowl, mix together the flour, polenta, caster sugar, bicarbonate of soda, baking powder, salt and three-quarters of the cherries, mixing well so that all the cherries are coated in the flour.

4. In a separate bowl or jug, stir together the lemon zest and juice, oil and milk. Make a well in the centre of the dry ingredients and pour in the wet. Slowly fold through the wet mixture, using a large spoon or spatula until fully combined.

5. Add the batter to the cake tin and smooth the top using the back of a spoon. Add the remaining cherries on top and sprinkle with the demerara sugar and almonds.

6. Bake for 35–40 minutes until a skewer inserted through the centre of the cake comes out clean.

7. Allow to cool for 10 minutes in the tin before removing from the tin to a wire rack. Delicious served slightly warm, or will keep in an airtight container for up to 5 days.

CHOCOLATE & CHESTNUT TORTE WITH HONEYCOMB

This features the flavours and textures of a Crunchie bar and it only takes seven ingredients to make! Use the best-quality vegan dark chocolate you can get as it'll make a huge difference to the final torte.

 SERVES 6   3 HRS

INGREDIENTS

- 150g vegan butter, plus extra for greasing
- 200g 70% vegan dark chocolate
- 1 x 200g pouch of Chestnut Purée
- 100g icing sugar
- Sea salt flakes
- Cocoa powder, to dust

For the honeycomb
- 150g caster sugar
- 3 tbsp golden syrup
- 1 1/2 tsp bicarbonate of soda

To serve
- Oat crème fraîche (optional)

METHOD

1. Grease the base and sides of a 20cm round loose-bottomed cake tin, then line with baking parchment.

2. Melt the chocolate in a bowl set over a pan of simmering water, making sure the bowl doesn't touch the water. Let the chocolate melt undisturbed for 2 minutes, then remove from the heat and stir so it's all evenly melted. Set aside to cool a little.

3. In a separate bowl, beat the butter, chestnut purée and icing sugar for 1–2 minutes until pale and fluffy. Carefully stir in the melted chocolate until evenly combined. Pour into the tin and smooth the top using the back of a spoon. Sprinkle with a little salt, then refrigerate for 1 hour (or overnight).

4. While the torte sets, make the honeycomb. Grease the base and sides of a 20cm round tin well. Heat the sugar and golden syrup in a deep, ideally non-stick, saucepan over a very gentle heat. Stir for a few minutes until the sugar has melted. The key is to not let the sugar bubble too much at this point.

5. Once all the sugar granules have dissolved, increase the heat slightly until the sugar starts to bubble a little – you want to very gently simmer the sugar for 1–2 minutes until you have a golden amber colour caramel. Working quickly, turn off the heat and add the bicarbonate of soda, beating it in quickly until there are no white patches left and the mixture is light, fluffy and foaming. Immediately pour the mixture into the prepared tin. Cool completely for 1 1/2 hours until the honeycomb has set.

6. Remove the torte from the fridge, lift it out of the tin and dust with cocoa powder. Run a knife under hot water, then slice the torte into 8 portions. Serve each slice with a crumble of honeycomb and a dollop of oat crème fraîche, if liked.

COCONUT RICE PUDDING

This is a sweet all-rounder that would be just as good for breakfast as it is after dinner.

 SERVES 4   25 MINS

INGREDIENTS

- 1 x 250g pouch of ready
  cooked Glorious Grains with
  Red Rice & Quinoa
- 1 x 400ml can full-fat
  coconut milk
- 1 tbsp light brown sugar,
  plus extra to serve

To serve
- 1 lime
- 1 mango, peeled and thinly
  sliced
- 1 tsp toasted sesame seeds

METHOD

1. Put the grains, coconut milk, sugar and 100ml water in a medium saucepan. Stir over a low heat for 15–20 minutes, or until thick and creamy and the grains are tender, adding a little more water if it needs a little longer.

2. Zest the lime, then with a small knife, cut off the peel and pith so that you are left with the inside of the lime. Cut out the segments of lime flesh, discarding the tough membrane. Add these to a bowl with the mango.

3. Serve large dollops of the coconut pudding with mango slices, lime segments, lime zest, sesame seeds and an extra sprinkling of brown sugar, to taste.

CHESTNUT & BANANA 'ICE CREAM'

For when you just need something sweet, healthy and really easy. If you like the sound of banoffee pie combined with a Snickers bar, then this one's for you. If you want to make this dessert a little more fancy for guests, serve with the chestnut praline from page 155.

 SERVES 4   2 HRS 10 MINS

INGREDIENTS

- 4 bananas, peeled and sliced
- 2 tbsp peanut butter
- 4 dates, pitted
- 1 x 180g pouch of ready cooked Whole Chestnuts

METHOD

1. Put the banana slices in a freezer bag or arrange on a tray in a single layer and place in the freezer for a minimum of 2 hours, or until completely frozen.

2. Put the frozen bananas in a blender with the peanut butter and dates and blend until smooth. You might have to stop the blender and stir everything a few times until the mixture becomes smooth and creamy.

3. Once it's nearly ready, add the chestnuts and blitz a few times until combined but you still have a few chunks of chestnut. Serve immediately.

CHOCOLATE TRAY BAKE WITH FROSTING

The lentils act as a second type of butter, resulting in a rich but light cake. You'll be so surprised that you can't taste the lentils at all!

 MAKES 16 SQUARES   50 MINS

INGREDIENTS

- 150g dark vegan chocolate
- 240g self-raising flour
- 40g cocoa powder
- 1 tsp bicarbonate of soda
- ½ tsp baking powder
- 1 x 250g pouch of ready cooked Beluga® Lentils
- 240g caster sugar
- 120g vegan baking margarine
- 450ml vegan milk

For the chocolate ganache
- 200ml coconut cream
- 250g vegan dark chocolate
- 2 tbsp coconut oil
- 150g icing sugar
- Pinch of sea salt flakes

METHOD

1. Preheat the oven to 160°C (140°C fan)/Gas mark 3.

2. Line a 27 x 20cm baking tray with parchment paper.

3. Break the chocolate into small, even pieces, then melt in a heatproof bowl over a pan of simmering water, making sure the water doesn't touch the bottom of the bowl. Stir a few times, then just before it's all melted, remove from the heat and allow to cool for 3–4 minutes.

4. Sift the flour, cocoa powder, bicarbonate of soda and baking powder into a mixing bowl and set aside.

5. In a food processor, add the lentils, sugar and vegan margarine and blitz for 1–2 minutes until really smooth and creamy. Pour in the milk and melted chocolate and blitz again until combined and you have a thin-looking batter.

6. Add the flour mixture and give it a final few pulses until all evenly combined and there are no clumps of flour.

7. Pour the batter into the tin and smooth the top using the back of a spoon. Bake for 30 minutes until firm on top. Remove from the oven and allow to cool in the tin for 15–30 minutes.

8. To make the chocolate ganache, gently heat the coconut cream in a saucepan until it just begins to simmer, then add the chocolate and coconut oil. Don't stir at this point; just leave to melt for 2 minutes, then stir until smooth. Now sift in the icing sugar and whisk until smooth. Allow to cool completely in the fridge.

9. Dollop the ganache onto the cake, spreading it out evenly. Sprinkle with the sea salt, then cut into 16 squares and serve.

QUINOA APPLE PIE

This is a crumble and an apple pie rolled into one. The quinoa in the base and topping provides a distinctive nutty flavour. It may seem like a lot of apples but they shrink once baked, so don't be afraid to pile them high.

 SERVES 6   1 HR 45 MINS

INGREDIENTS

For the quinoa base
- 1 x 250g pouch of ready cooked Red & White Quinoa
- 50g hazelnuts
- 2 tbsp caster sugar
- 175g plain flour, plus extra for dusting
- 125g cold vegan butter, cut into small pieces, plus extra for greasing

For the topping
- 65g vegan butter
- 50g jumbo oats
- 50g chopped nuts (hazelnuts, pecans or almonds)
- 3 tbsp demerara sugar

For the filling
- 4–5 medium cooking apples, cored and roughly chopped
- 3 tbsp caster sugar
- 1 tsp ground cinnamon
- Juice of ½ lemon

To serve
- Vegan vanilla ice cream

METHOD

1. Add 150g of the quinoa, the hazelnuts, caster sugar and flour to a food processor and blitz to a fine crumb. Add the vegan butter and pulse a few times until you have a rough dough.

2. Tip the pastry out onto a floured surface and gather into a ball, then wrap in clingfilm and chill in the fridge for 30 minutes.

3. Preheat the oven to 200°C (180°C fan)/Gas mark 6.

4. Grease the base and sides of a 22cm round pie dish or cake tin. On a sheet of parchment paper, roll out the pastry into a circle 2cm thick and a few cm larger than your pie dish. Lift up the paper and pastry and carefully invert into the dish. Peel off the paper (reserve it) and push the pastry neatly into all the edges and up the sides. Trim off any excess around the top. Prick the base a few times with a fork.

5. Add the parchment back on top of the base, then pour in some baking beans and blind bake for 15 minutes. Remove the beans and the paper, then bake for another 10 minutes until golden.

6. To make the topping, add the remaining quinoa, butter, jumbo oats, nuts and demerara sugar to the food processor and pulse a few times until you have a crumbly mixture.

7. To make the filling, toss the apples in the sugar, cinnamon and lemon juice then tumble into the base.

8. Sprinkle the topping over the apples, then bake for 30–40 minutes until the apples are soft and the top is golden. Serve with vegan vanilla ice cream.

CHESTNUT & CHOCOLATE MOUSSE

This is the best vegan chocolate mousse – the chestnut purée and aquafaba make it so light and airy and highly addictive. Serve either in a large serving bowl or in small glasses.

 SERVES 6–8   1 HR 30 MINS

INGREDIENTS

- 1 x 200g pouch of Chestnut Purée
- 200g good-quality vegan dark chocolate, roughly chopped
- 2–4 tbsp freshly boiled water
- Aquafaba from 1 x 400g can chickpeas (150ml)
- 100g caster sugar
- 2 tbsp of cocoa powder
- Sea salt flakes
- 100ml vegan cream

To serve
- Seasonal berries
- Handful of toasted hazelnuts, pecans, pistachios or almonds, roughly chopped

METHOD

1. Empty the chestnut purée from the pouch into a bowl and stir until smooth.

2. Add the chocolate and half the chestnut purée to a heatproof bowl over a small saucepan of simmering water, making sure the bottom of the bowl doesn't touch the water. Don't stir for the first few minutes, then stir and remove from the heat for the rest of the chocolate to melt.

3. Loosen the chocolate and chestnut mixture by adding the boiled water a little at a time, stirring until smooth and glossy.

4. In a stand mixer or using an electric hand whisk, whisk the aquafaba for 4–5 minutes until it forms stiff peaks. Add the sugar a little at a time and whisk for 3–4 minutes until the mixture is soft and glossy, like a loose meringue.

5. Very carefully fold the melted chocolate and cocoa powder into the meringue until fully combined and no more white streaks are visible.

6. Spoon the mixture into a large serving bowl or 6–8 glasses, sprinkle with a little sea salt and chill in the fridge for a minimum of 1 hour.

7. Before serving, make the chestnut cream. Whisk together the remaining half of the chestnut purée and the cream until smooth and pour into a small bowl or jug.

8. Serve the mousse with the chestnut cream, fresh berries and toasted nuts.

CHESTNUT SHORTBREAD WITH ROAST STRAWBERRIES

This works so well with many types of fruit, so you can swap the strawberries for whatever is in season, bearing in mind that stone fruits such as greengages, plums and apricots take a little longer to roast. This makes a big batch of shortbread because it keeps really well and is perfect to give to friends.

 SERVES 4–6   1 HR

INGREDIENTS

For the shortbread
- 225g vegan butter
- 1 x 180g pouch of ready cooked Whole Chestnuts
- 300g plain flour
- 120g caster sugar, plus 2 tbsp, for sprinkling
- Pinch of sea salt

For the roast strawberries
- 450g strawberries, halved or quartered
- Zest and juice of 1 lemon
- 2 tbsp caster sugar

To serve
- Oat crème fraîche or thick vegan Greek-style yogurt

METHOD

1. For the shortbread, scoop teaspoon-sized balls of the vegan butter into a bowl and freeze for a minimum of 15 minutes to get it as cold as possible while you prepare everything else. This will really help get a crumbly texture.

2. Add the chestnuts to a food processor and pulse a few times until roughly chopped. Remove half and set aside, then add the flour, sugar and salt to the food processor and pulse again a few times just to sift the flour.

3. Now add the cold butter and pulse again until the mixture resembles chunky breadcrumbs; you don't want a full dough, so don't overmix. Tip the mixture into a 22cm round or square baking tin lined with baking paper. Very lightly press the reserved chestnuts into the mixture until you have a smooth-ish surface. Refrigerate for 15 minutes, or until ready to bake. This can be done up to 24 hours before baking.

4. Preheat the oven to 180°C (160°C fan)/Gas mark 4. Mix the strawberries, lemon zest and juice and sugar in a large roasting tin. Spread out the strawberries into a single layer and roast in the oven for 5–7 minutes until the juices start to caramelise around the edges of the tin. Remove from the oven and spoon into a bowl to cool slightly.

5. When you're ready, bake the shortbread for 15–20 minutes (you can do this at the same time as the strawberries) until lightly golden on top, then remove from the oven and sprinkle with the sugar. Allow to rest for 5 minutes before cutting it into portions. It helps to cut it while slightly warm.

6. Serve with a large dollop of oat crème fraîche or vegan Greek-style yogurt.

AQUAFABA MERINGUES WITH A CHESTNUT PRALINE & POACHED RHUBARB

The chestnut praline is very addictive, so try not to finish the lot before you serve the meringue! The rhubarb is the perfect sour accompaniment to the sweet meringue, but so many fruits work with this – just poach whatever's in season.

 SERVES 8   6 HRS

INGREDIENTS

For the meringues
- Aquafaba from 1 x 400g can chickpeas (150ml)
- Tiny pinch of salt
- 200g golden caster sugar (or regular caster sugar)
- 1½ tsp cream of tartar
- 1 tsp vanilla paste

For the chestnut praline
- 100g mixed pecans, hazelnuts, almonds and/or pistachios
- 1 x 180g pouch of ready cooked Whole Chestnuts
- 300g caster sugar
- Sea salt

For the poached rhubarb
- 500g rhubarb, sliced into 4cm pieces
- 2 tbsp caster sugar

METHOD

1. Preheat the oven to 100°C (80°C fan)/Gas mark ¼. Line 2 baking trays with baking paper.

2. Whisk the aquafaba with the salt in a stand mixer for 5–6 minutes until stiff. In a bowl, combine the sugar and cream of tartar. Once the aquafaba is stiff, continue whisking and add the sugar mixture, 1 teaspoon at a time, followed by the vanilla paste, and whisk for a further 2–4 minutes until you have soft, glossy peaks and the sugar has dissolved.

3. Spoon 4 large dollops of meringue, 5cm apart, onto each of the baking trays. Make an indent in the middle using a tablespoon so the sides are a little higher than the middle. Bake for 2 hours until firm on top. Turn off the heat and let dry in the oven with the door ajar for 4 hours or overnight.

4. For the chestnut praline, toast the nuts and chestnuts in a heavy-based saucepan over a medium heat for 5 minutes, then tip them into a bowl. In the same pan, gently melt the sugar on a medium–low heat, without stirring, until a deep golden colour. If you need to, you can tip the pan a little to allow the sugar to melt evenly. Add the pecans and chestnuts and stir to coat, then pour onto a non-stick baking tray or a tray greased with a flavourless oil. Sprinkle with a little sea salt, then allow to cool completely. Chop into small pieces.

5. To poach the rhubarb, add the pieces to a wide pan with the sugar and 50ml of water and simmer for 8 minutes until soft but not falling apart. Remove from the heat.

6. To assemble, place a few pieces of rhubarb next to each meringue and top with the praline.

CHESTNUT & PLUM TARTE TATIN

Apples are usually the queen of this dessert, but the tartness from the plums is particularly delicious with the sweet chestnut paste. Feel free to use any stone fruit that's available.

 SERVES 6   35 MINS

INGREDIENTS

- 5–6 ripe fresh plums, halved and stoned
- 15g vegan butter
- 2 tbsp caster sugar
- 1 x 320g vegan ready-rolled puff pastry sheet

Chestnut paste
- 1 x 200g pouch of Chestnut Purée
- 2 tbsp caster sugar
- 20g vegan butter

To serve
- Vegan vanilla ice cream

METHOD

1. Preheat the oven to 200°C (180°C fan)/Gas mark 6.

2. Place the plums, cut side down, in a 23cm heavy-based ovenproof frying pan. Place over medium heat and add the vegan butter and sugar. Heat for 4 minutes, gently pushing the plums around every so often, or until the sugar has dissolved and the plums are starting to soften on the bottom.

3. Cut the puff pastry into a circle the size of your pan – cutting around a similar-sized plate is a good way to do this.

4. For the chestnut paste, mix the chestnut purée, sugar and vegan butter into a paste, then spread evenly over the pastry base all the way to the edge.

5. Carefully but confidentally flip the pastry over onto the plums in the pan so that the uncoated side of the pastry is facing up.

6. Bake for 20–25 minutes until the pastry is crisp and puffed up and the plums are soft underneath.

7. Remove from the oven and leave to cool for a few minutes in the pan. Now get a plate that's larger than the pan and invert it over the pan. Holding plate and pan together tightly, quickly but carefully flip everything over, making sure no hot juices seep out and burn you. Don't worry if a few plums are stuck to the pan – just prise them off and replace on the tart.

8. Serve warm with a scoop of vegan vanilla ice cream.

INDEX

Published in 2021 by Quadrille,
an imprint of Hardie Grant Publishing

Quadrille
52–54 Southwark Street
London SE1 1UN
quadrille.com

Publishing Director Sarah Lavelle
Senior Commissioning Editor Céline Hughes
Designers Emily Lapworth & Gemma Hayden
Cover Designer Uncommon Creative Studio
Recipe Developer and Food Stylist Kitty Coles
Photographer Kim Lightbody
Prop Stylist Luis Peral
Production Controller Sinead Hering
Head of Production Stephen Lang

Merchant Gourmet
2 Rollins Street
London SE15 1EW
www.merchant-gourmet.com

Brand Manager Caroline Moore
Head of Brand Nyree Chambers

Cataloguing in Publication
Data: a catalogue record for
this book is available from
the British Library.

Photography, text, design and
layout © Quadrille 2021

Reprinted in 2022
10 9 8 7 6 5 4 3 2

ISBN 978-1-78713-761-5

Printed in China